Garrow's Law

The BBC Drama Revisited

John Hostettler

Garrow's Law
The BBC Drama Revisited
John Hostettler

ISBN 978-1-904380-90-0 (Paperback)
ISBN 978-1-908162-22-9 (Kindle/Epub)
ISBN 978-1-908162-23-6 (Adobe Ebook)

Published 2012 by

Waterside Press Ltd. **Telephone** +44(0)1256 882250
Sherfield Gables **E-mail** enquiries@watersidepress.co.uk
Sherfield-on-Loddon **Online catalogue** WatersidePress.co.uk
Hook, Hampshire
United Kingdom RG27 0JG

UK distributor Gardners Books, 1 Whittle Drive, Eastbourne, East Sussex, BN23 6QH. Tel: +44 (0)1323 521777; sales@gardners.com; www.gardners.com

Copyright © 2012 This work is the copyright of John Hostettler. All intellectual property and associated rights are hereby asserted and reserved by the author in full compliance with UK, European and international law. No part of this book may be copied, reproduced, stored in any retrieval system or transmitted in any form or by any means, including in hard copy or via the internet, without the prior written permission of the publishers to whom all such rights have been assigned worldwide. The *Preface* in the copyright of Bryan Gibson © 2012.

Cover design © 2012 Waterside Press. Original pastel of William Garrow by John Russell RA reproduced by kind permission of owner and Garrow family member Arthur Crawfurd. Design by www.gibgob.com

Cataloguing-In-Publication Data A catalogue record for this book can be obtained from the British Library.

e-book *Garrow's Law* is available as an e-book and also to subscribers of Myilibrary and Dawsonera.

Printed by Lightning Source.

Garrow's Law
The BBC Drama Revisited

John Hostettler

Preface Bryan Gibson

✻ WATERSIDE PRESS

Contents

Acknowledgments ... vii
About the Author ... ix
Preface ... xi

Part 1: Crime and Law in the 18th Century   25

1. Garrow's Gift to the World   27
    Airbrushed Out of History ... 27
    Background to the TV Series ... 28
    The Rights of Defendants ... 29
    "Old Bailey Hacks" ... 30
    Adversary Trial ... 32
    The "No-Counsel" Rule ... 34
    The Lawyers Capture the Courtroom ... 35
    Rules of Criminal Evidence ... 36

2. Eighteenth Century London Life   41
    Teeming Population ... 41
    Absence of a Police Force ... 42
    Felonies ... 43
    The Old Bailey ... 45
    Benefit of Clergy ... 46
    Coachmaker's Hall ... 47
    Advocate ... 48

Part 2: Reality and Dramatic Invention — 51

3. "Garrow's Law" — 53

BBC1 53
TV Series 1 54
Garrow's First Case 54
Infanticide 56
Duelling 58
"Sweepings" 58
London's Monster 59
Lady Sarah Dore 61
A Case of Rape 62
Thief-takers 64
High Treason 66
Garrow and Erskine 69

4. TV Series 2 — 71

Amicus Curiae *71*
The Zong Slave Ship 72
Sodomy 73

The Seamen's Hospital Case	74
Erskine's Guinea	75
Injustice for Children	76
Criminal Conversation	77

5. TV Series 3   81

The Deranged Soldier	81
Pious Perjury	84
Pro Bono Publico Work ("Work for the Public Good")	87
Dispute with the Bench	89
Torture in Trinidad—The Picton Trial	92
Moral Issue of Slavery	94
Death on the Hustings	95

6. Afterword   97

Coal Face of Legal History	97

Glossary 1: Judicial and Historical Terms in use in Garrow's Time   101

Glossary 2: Capital Offences Tried Frequently at the Old Bailey in Garrow's Time   107

Bibliogaphy   113

Index   117

Acknowledgments

I am grateful to Arthur Crawfurd for permission to use for the cover of this book his original 1783 pastel of William Garrow believed to be by John Russell RA. Russell was an English painter renowned for his portraits in oils and pastels who portrayed many of Garrow's family. This, probably unique image, shows the young Garrow at the time he commenced upon his remarkable career at the Old Bailey wearing his newly-acquired barrister's wig.

Arthur Crawfurd is connected to Garrow twice. First, Garrow's son, the Reverend Dr David William Garrow, married Charlotte Caroline Proby. Her elder sister, Arabella, married Charles Payne Crawfurd of Saint Hill, near East Grinstead, Sussex.

Secondly, David William and Charlotte had a daughter, Georgina Laetitia who married Robert Crawfurd the son of Arabella and Charles. Georgina Laetitia was Robert's second wife and they were first cousins. They married in middle age and had no children. Arthur Crawfurd is descended from Robert Crawfurd and his first wife, Patty Stutter.

I should also like to thank Richard Braby who kindly read the manuscript of this book and made a number of useful suggestions for its improvement. I have incorporated these but, needless to say, any errors that remain are entirely my responsibility.

John Hostettler
October 2012

About the Author

John Hostettler was a practising solicitor in London for 35 years as well as undertaking political and civil liberties cases in Nigeria, Germany and Aden. He sat as a magistrate for a number of years and has also been a chairman of tribunals. He played a leading role in the abolition of flogging in British colonial prisons and served on a Home Office Committee to revise the rules governing electoral law in Britain. He holds several university degrees and three doctorates. *Garrow's Law: The BBC Drama Revisited* is his 22nd book.

His biographical works include those on the radical social reformer Thomas Wakley and legal icons Sir James Fitzjames Stephen, Sir Edward Carson, Sir Edward Coke, Lord Halsbury and Sir Matthew Hale. His last book, *Dissenters, Radicals, Heretics and Blasphemers: The Flame of Revolt that Shines Through English History* is being entered for the Orwell Prize.

John Hostettler's writings encompass a succession of other acclaimed works, including *The Criminal Jury Old and New: Jury Power from Early Times to the Present Day*; *Fighting for Justice: The History and Origins of Adversary Trial*; *Hanging in the Balance: A History of the Abolition of Capital Punishment in Britain* (with Brian P Block and a Foreword by former Prime Minister Lord Callaghan); *A History of Criminal Justice in England and Wales*; *Champions of the Rule of Law* and *Sir Thomas Erskine*.

In 2009, his book *Sir William Garrow: His Life, Times and Fight for Justice*, co-authored with Richard Braby (a descendant of William

Garrow), rescued from obscurity the true story of one of English law's forgotten legal giants, a tale mirrored by the prime-time BBC TV series "Garrow's Law" with which this new work is concerned.

The author of the Preface

Bryan Gibson is the founder of Waterside Press and also of the Garrow Society (with others). A barrister-at-law, he has written various books on different aspects of criminal justice.

Preface

I hope this book will be of interest to anyone who saw the BBC series "Garrow's Law" as well as to others who care about legal institutions. Written by expert commentator John Hostettler, it compares fact and fiction in the life of the lawyer William Garrow.

In *Part I* John looks at the day-to-day world in which Garrow worked, marking out those aspects of crime and punishment which served to deal with "troublesome" members of society, mainly deprived and underprivileged people. These unfortunates fed the conveyor belt to the courts, prisons and gallows. It was a world in which life was cheap, rights scant, and in which the machinery of justice ensured rapid and effortless convictions, ready condemnation, draconian punishments and widespread prejudice.

This is the backdrop against which TV audiences were, in 2009, introduced to the story of the individual who set out to change the legal world. Juxtaposition of judicial sway, procedural chaos, a baying public gallery and impudence in the face of authority fired the public imagination as Garrow sought ever more ingenious ways of avoiding legal rules. At the time, e.g. these prevented the accused's counsel from speaking directly to the jury, visiting a client in prison to take instructions, or knowing about the prosecution evidence in advance of it being given from the witness box.

In *Part II*, the author works his way through the cases portrayed in the TV series explaining their true origins and the real life jigsaw of facts, roles and events which the scriptwriters, led by Tony

Marchant, and others such as consultant Mark Pallis and Dominic Barlow of Twenty-Twenty Productions, wrestled with in the interests of dramatic effect. He tells also how, in reality, the law had its own peculiar fictions — such as "pious perjury" — a device invented by juries to prevent accused people from being completely subjugated, browbeaten and led-off to their appalling ends.

A Radical and a Rebel

It is a matter of intrigue how Garrow—famous in his own day, then lost to the world—returned to prominence due to modern media, so that he is nowadays as much at home on TV, Google and BlackBerry, or in tweets and other instant messages, as he is in the history books. This is largely due to the success of the prime-time BBC 1 series, or three series in fact, those of 2009, 2010 and 2011.

Each episode attracted over five million viewers on a Sunday evening (and some of the programmes have been broadcast again at various times as well as in places like the USA and Australia). In the 12 episodes, Garrow is portrayed as an anti-establishment hero, a protagonist of bold new ideas at odds with the conventions, courtesies and sometimes mystical ways of the English Bar. He was a radical and a rebel, fighting what in modern parlance is known as "noble cause corruption", i.e. where the person bending the rules or taking short-cuts does so in the mistaken belief that they are doing the right thing. He had to deal with domineering judges, compliant witnesses, habitual jurors (whose regular attendance in the same jury box tended to make them prosecution-minded) and wickeder abuses.

Much of this book is about the differences between "reality and dramatic invention". One thing we do know and were introduced to early on in the TV series is that Garrow had a particular dislike of thief-takers, whose livelihood depended on seeing as many convictions and rewards as possible, and "guinea men" who would swear to anything for a fee. It was an evil trade in false testimony and vested interest whereby lawyers and others connected to the justice system were tempted, out of self-interest, to stay quiet and keep in line. So "Garrow's Law" is also a morality tale of sorts, a warning about just how wrapped-up in its own ambitions any set-up can become — even, in Garrow's time, if this meant someone being executed at Tyburn or outside Newgate Prison.

Airbrushed from History

Garrow broke the mould and tried to re-shape matters. As might be expected this attracted enemies in both the underworld of 18th century Britain and detractors in its ruling class as well as from his own profession. But who was he? Even before the first episode was broadcast, "Garrow's Law" was being featured in the *Radio Times* and national press, the former stating for our edification:

> Without the pioneering work of William Garrow, the legal system would still be stuck in the Middle Ages.

So how and why was William Garrow airbrushed from history only to be rescued by a tentative publication (of which more later) and modern-day technology such as TV, social media and online records from the Old Bailey and other public institutions. This in itself is a whodunnit. Maybe "his face didn't fit", "he was a rank outsider" or had "ruffled the feathers of the political elite". It is common knowledge that he was dubbed the "Billingsgate Boy" by some of his contemporaries, not least in the TV series on his very first day in court by prosecuting counsel John Silvester.

Garrow was famous in his day, to wit various portraits (some reproduced in their hundreds like 17th-century cigarette cards, if mostly lost) and his name appears regularly in the newspapers and law reports. Then he disappears from the collective memory.

The TV series hints at how, at the height of his reforming powers as an advocate, Garrow was placated with a knighthood, but it does not cover his subsequent election as an MP, appointment as Solicitor-General and then Attorney-General, prosecuting in the latter capacity on behalf of the state in historic treason trials at a time when there was great fear of revolution spreading from the continent to Britain. At this he turned out to be mediocre and less successful than as an up-and-coming defence advocate. As a judge, he is remembered for no great legal wisdom, though he did continue to build on the ideas he had promulgated as an energetic and highly motivated young barrister, before fading into obscurity.

There is another moral here — "Stick to what you are good at!" Garrow may have been a celebrated advocate but he was undistinguished in high office. Trading his true principles to join the establishment, to which he never really belonged, may have had something to do with being "forgotten". It is, of course, the free-spirited Garrow of his youth that makes for such riveting viewing.

A Breath of Fresh Air

I first became aware of William Garrow in 2004 when John Hostettler included an outline of his contribution to English law in a manuscript he sent me called *Fighting for Justice: The Origins and History of Adversary Trial* (it was later published under that title). There John wrote:

> Garrow was a consummate advocate ... unrivalled in the art of cross-examination, and such was his power at the Bar that he was

> appointed King's Counsel ... All his successes ... and his lasting achievements had been won in the short period of ten years.

It is always refreshing to happen across something new and I was drawn in by the story of this upstart lawyer who breezed through the courts in assertive (even aggressive) mode, sacrificing sacred cows as he did so. I was not immediately convinced that Garrow's ten years in court justified an entire chapter, but I took it John knew the importance of the man. It was that early chapter which triggered a chain of events which led to the BBC programmes. In the meantime, however, John had embarked on an altogether more ambitious project. He was writing not just a chapter about Garrow, but an entire book — working tirelessly on Garrow's rehabilitation!

A Remarkable Output

John has written a small library of biographical (and other) works on great lawyers and jurists. They mostly concern famous people, household names (at least within legal households), well-known judges and jurists like Edward Coke, Matthew Hale, Henry Brougham, Cesare Beccaria, Lord Halsbury and Edward Carson. And he had already, some years earlier, written a book on one lawyer from the same era as Garrow whose face clearly did fit the politics of the day and the story handed down by scholars and tutors. Thomas Erskine QC *was* remembered by lawyers, historians and academics alike and took considerable credit for legal developments, sometimes at Garrow's expense.

Thomas Erskine crops up in the TV series, including as Garrow's duly-respected opponent in a case in which he, Garrow, was personally involved. Interestingly, as this book explains, in the series the roles of Garrow and Erskine are sometimes reversed in the interests of the drama, to make sure, e.g. that Garrow ends up on the winning side or attracts the sympathy of the viewer.

So I had no hesitation in taking on John's earlier work in progress as he continued to research Garrow in the archives — if only on the basis of his track record. In short, I knew from experience that it would be a first-class account. What I also knew was that the manuscript would arrive on time, polished and with little need for in-house editing. Few people have the knowledge and skills to write for the published page first time out.

If it is said nowhere else, I should remedy this right here by recording the debt of gratitude that generations of students of English legal and social history owe to John. It is comforting to think that his more than 20 works will exist for future reference not just in libraries but also cyberspace due to developments such as e-books, Kindle and modern developments whereby books can be printed remotely at the touch of a button, from an electronic file, for delivery across large parts of the world.

Joining Forces

The decision to publish was helped by the news that Richard Braby, a descendant of Garrow's in America was happy to collaborate and become co-author. Never mind if the result was no more than a worthy tome to grace the shelves of libraries, die-hard collectors and genealogists. To the main title, *Sir William Garrow,* was added *His Life, Times and Fight for Justice* — in an unashamed attempt to cultivate broader interest.

So it is John *and* Richard who are to be credited with "bringing Garrow in from the cold". Others have written about him, to be sure, notably the historians John M Beattie and Richard Vogler who are experts on that era of legal history — articles, passages, contributions — and latterly others have written scripts, but nothing to equal the wealth of factual and family-based information that emerged as a result of John and Richard's collaboration.

I now find Garrow cropping up in other works in a way which suggests he has been known about in certain circles for some time, such as that of Gregory Durston of Kingston University, who cites Beattie's work as one of his sources and provides yet another perspective on those times.[1] Another author to mention Garrow but in a different context is Muriel Whitten who focused on his involvement with philanthropists and the anti-slavery movement.[2]

The "rediscovered" William Garrow of John and Richard's book was soon basking in the reflected glory of his larger than life TV alter-ego, courtesy of dramatic licence, role changes, "some facts altered" and a secret love affair with an attractive woman, with the added frisson that this was across the same social divide which separated Garrow from the exclusivity of the world he challenged (and in his youth despised). The squalor of Newgate Prison, goal fever and poverty today, the grand houses, expensive clothes, cut-glass chandeliers, servants, polished surfaces and fine wines tomorrow. Who can blame William in the TV series when he walks out of a dinner-party after one put-down too many, having exhausted his tolerance of "the discreet charm of the bourgeoisie".

Every Lawyer's Boxed-set

Garrow, who when not offending the sensitivities of his "betters", was busy in the courtroom or chambers, burning the midnight oil,

---

[1]. See *Whores and Highwaymen: Crime and Justice in the Eighteenth Century Metropolis*, Waterside Press, 2012.
[2]. See *Nipping Crime in the Bud: How the Philanthropic Quest was Put into Law,* Waterside Press, 2010.

honing his "gifts to the world" — including the presumption of innocence, a better relationship between judge and jury (the former having until then overawed juries), rules of evidence and the right to a defence lawyer — was successfully portrayed on screen by the actor Andrew Buchan. His mentor and guide, William Southouse (formerly thought to be called "Thomas" and in the BBC series styled "John") was played by Alun Armstrong.

The strong cast also included Lyndsey Marshall as Lady Sarah Hill (in real life the future Mrs Garrow who in truth was never married to Hill and only latterly to Garrow after an "irregular relationship"). Sarah Dore, to use her real name, remains an enigma despite many lines of enquiry.

Rupert Graves played Sir Arthur Hill and Michael Culkin a bucolic, overbearing, yet at times friendly and even supportive, Judge Buller. After the initial shock of encountering the newcomer Garrow, Buller seems to have warmed to him in his own irascible way. Buller was in reality "Sir Francis" or "Mr Justice" Buller, a High Court judge responsible for many sittings at the Old Bailey in its capacity as the Assize court for London. According to Mark Pallis, the storyline consultant to "Garrow's Law", Buller was the judge immortalised by cartoonist James Gilray after Buller ruled, in 1782, that "It is acceptable to beat one's wife, so long as the stick is no bigger than one's thumb". Some people say this gave rise to the expression "rule of thumb". What an epitaph!

Indeed, the story of William Garrow is a vehicle for all manner of surprising discoveries about the people or facts lurking beneath the drama and many of the themes carry messages far beyond that of an everyday TV programme as John Hostettler shows in this book.

Missing Link

John and Richard's earlier work — their *magnum opus* — assured people that Garrow *is* the missing link in the development of adversary trial and aspects of English law of the kind I have already mentioned. As Geoffrey Robertson QC (the epitome of a modern-day Garrow in terms of his fearlessness about taking on challenging or unpopular causes) wrote in the Foreword:

> Garrow can be truly said to have revolutionised the practice of criminal law.

The wheel is still in spin, of course. Today there can sometimes be a political backlash against hard won rights of individuals, which belies how easily regimes can escalate into forms of repression or worse. We see it in countries around the world to this day; whilst in the UK what are almost, nowadays, everyday disclosures concerning some or other malpractice that has been unearthed should act as a red light. On the other hand, the general direction is still one of huge progress and understanding of a kind that was sadly lacking when Garrow first took up the cudgels.

Forensic Skills, Adversary Trial and Conflict

Drama and the real life practice of cross-examination are good bedfellows. Much of the tension in "Garrow's Law" stems from those scenes in which Garrow dissects the evidence of an unreliable, untruthful or hostile witness. This and powerful speeches to the jury (or, in Garrow's time, as John Hostettler points out, words routed via the judge's ears to the jurors or by way of asides) are a dramatic convention used to propel stories forward.

The merits of adversary trial can sometimes be contentious with those of a modern-day, restorative persuasion, who see conflict resolution as less divisive. Garrow was hardly a natural mediator and traditional cross-examination is hardly the subtle approach of the problem solver, bridge builder or hostage negotiator.

I occasionally find myself defending Garrow to proponents of restorative justice — we must have published a dozen such books over the years — whilst at the same time championing the merits of the kind of trial which Garrow forged, in which two sides engage in a contest using tactics and manoeuvres.

John's own answer is that adversary trial and restorative approaches are complementary; and indeed, in the end result, outstanding issues of dispute can only be resolved by some system that allows for disagreement, debate and the systematic resolution of competing points of view. Rules are needed for this and it was Garrow's work which led to those concerning criminal procedure and evidence which allowed for a fair trial and conflict to be resolved in a properly structured way. It is also true that, in its modern form, adversary trial places the onus very much on the prosecutor and for this we must be grateful to Garrow and his contemporaries. There are intimations of how all this came about in the TV series.

Who was William Garrow?

We have come a long way from the beer-garden atmosphere of the courts where Garrow practised, the perfect backdrop for 'factional' enhancements, cut-and-thrust action and flights of imagination. Thankfully, the viewing public know what they like. The BAFTA nominated and Royal Television Society Award-winning programme for Best History went on air just as John and Richard's book was released and the effect was electrifying. What had begun as a modest project — a labour of love with few pretensions beyond the project's inherent worth — took off beyond all expectations. Hooked on the TV series, millions of viewers and thousands of readers demanded to know more about Garrow and an unplanned campaign began for his rehabilitation—accompanied by a detectable shift in the level of debate around issues of crime and punishment.

Until then the situation can be typified by considering a number of reactions to advance trailing of the book and programme:

- "Has anybody heard of William Garrow?" (*Law Society Gazette*);

- "Even though I have taken a keen interest in legal history... I was not aware of William Garrow" (Clive Anderson writing in the *Daily Telegraph*); and

- "Hmm, thought so... all that will now change" (Frances Gibb, *The Times*).

Within weeks of the first episode being broadcast, many more people were asking, "Who was William Garrow?"

In the intriguing way that word-of-mouth travels, it became *de rigueur* to feign surprise and admit to a lack of existing knowledge about the individual who had done so much for English law. Except, that is, for a few historians (such as those already mentioned) and in and around the Inns of Court: Lincoln's Inn in particular, where Garrow was a bencher and his portrait hangs in some splendour, if until recently largely un-remarked upon.

It also fascinated people that Garrow was a great informal debater. The idea of jumping up onto one's chair and addressing the assembled throng, hoping to convince them that black is white seems to sum up Garrow perfectly—the power of persuasion, winning over a sceptical audience—whether the crowd be in the public bar, the courtroom, Parliament, Gray's Inn (my own Inn of Court where the convention of after dinner "challenges" of a similar kind persists) or Hyde Park Corner.

Turning the tide when faced with an impossible brief: here Garrow as fiction was a clear winner, and in real life, though not infallible, someone who won his audience over more times than not. As John explains, the originally somewhat timid Garrow forged his ability for public speaking in the spit and sawdust of crowded taverns where impromptu arguments — "spouting" — were commonplace.

The Garrow Society

Demand for greater information about Garrow's life and times led to the formation of the online Garrow Society (see garrowsociety. org) of which John, Richard and myself are founder members. It is a free internet-based resource and attracts queries and information from around the world. It was party to an official blue plaque being placed on Garrow's home in Pegwell Bay, Kent after it joined forces with the local Ramsgate Society to press the authorities into action.

Pegwell Cottage, is now owned by a rather grand lady called Alma Beattie (no relation to John M Beattie above), who is the proprietor of a holiday caravan site in its grounds. It is a fine building on a cliff overlooking the English Channel. It was on a biting cold day, with snow in the air, that John and I unveiled the plaque for the watching media, later reporting back to Richard in America about this encouraging development. At the same time Garrow's grave was tidied-up and conducted tours began in the churchyard of St Lawrence, Ramsgate. Garrow's London Home by the Houses of Parliament is long demolished.

Increasingly at the website, people started to compare the real life

Garrow with his fictional "avatar" and to ask questions about the cases in which he acted and in particular his relationship with Sarah Dore, the love interest in the TV series, with whom there seems to be endless fascination. Comparisons between TV and reality abound in this book, as marshalled by John, who also managed to appear in an explanatory video made by the producers of "Garrow's Law" which became part of their DVD package.

Amongst the themes and issues pursued by the Garrow Society are: the infamous trial of General Picton; details of Garrow's family; the treatment of women and children (an issue pertinent throughout the drama); the search for information about Sarah Dore; as well as historical articles about Garrow's life and times and further comparisons with the TV series.

There are to be sure, many Garrows, whether of that exact name or not but certainly of that line and pedigree, around the British Isles and the world to this day — a veritable dynasty. A number of them contacted us with information or questions, whilst images of or connected to Garrow began to surface from divers attics, including the fine portrait by John Russell RA (so we believe) on the cover of this book, courtesy of Garrow relative Arthur Crawfurd. Other people have come forward having ploughed a lonely furrow over many years. One such is mentioned by John in a footnote in *Chapter 1*, Ann Bremner who gave us proof that Southouse was called William and not Thomas. This was accepted by the *Dictionary of National Biography* and related entries amended accordingly.

It always astounds me the connections that lie to be discovered through publishing biography or history (I recall once a man introducing himself to me at one book launch as the great great nephew of Thomas Wooldridge the trooper executed at Reading Gaol who was the subject of Oscar Wilde's fine ballad; a West Country solicitor contacting me following an article I wrote about John Lee,

"The man they could not hang", to say that his firm was the one that acted for Lee in the 1800s; not to mention random people who simply want to add to the bank of knowledge on a given subject).

Another image of Garrow is the black and white mezzotint which we used on the cover of the paperback edition of *Sir William Garrow* in which he looks not unlike how Andrew Buchan portrays him in "Garrow's Law", which I came upon by chance in the art dealers Sanders of Oxford. I left it to be parcelled-up for the journey home and when I returned to collect it the owner, sensing that he may have missed a trick, asked, quizically, "Is that the guy in the TV programme?" It has pride of place in my study and is the only copy I know of to have survived apart from that in the National Gallery.

The British Psyche

Above all there seems to be something "very British" about William Garrow, the non-conformist lawyer whose roots lie in Scotland. This, I think, is at the core of interest in him. His legend also plays off the opposite stereotypes of out-of-touch judges, corrupt officials and cavalier practitioners. He revels in reversals of fortune — and something else that chimes is the notion that he had little knowledge of the law, or at least if he did he kept this to himself, knowing perhaps that human nature prefers modesty to cleverness (in fact Garrow wrote a standard text book in law French). Such devices are the lifeblood of "Garrow's Law", spawning interest, illusion and magic.

Running side-by-side, is the lost story of Garrow and its rediscovery after 200 plus years. He did not win every time whether in real life or on the TV screen: but he has been won back for posterity.

Bryan Gibson
October 2012

Part 1

Crime and Law in the 18th Century

Chapter 1

Garrow's Gift to the World

Airbrushed Out of History

On a dark night in November 2009 a fresh costume drama made its debut on several million TV screens throughout the United Kingdom. Entitled "Garrow's Law", it portrayed the first dramatic ten years of the ascendancy at the Old Bailey of the most celebrated and successful defence lawyer William Garrow. By this means three BBC prime-time television series brought Garrow alive for millions of people for the first time.

An outline of his breath-taking achievements at the Old Bailey in eighteenth century London flashed into people's homes in the opening shots and revealed in courtroom scenes that fired the imagination against a background of the vivid and colourful scenario of London life of the time.

In the interests of drama and tension, however, fiction was mixed in with fact. As Tony Marchant, co-creator of the series, said,

> I invented and extemporised on what is known to make an interesting drama.

Although he did add that "you have to be truthful". What I would like to consider here is how far the programmes showed the reality of the revolution in criminal law that, almost single-handedly, Garrow created over two hundred years ago and that still affects our lives today.

Background to the TV Series

When the series commenced, a viewer might well have asked, "Who is Garrow?" As the well-known barrister Clive Anderson put it, "Even though I have taken a keen interest in criminal legal history before… I was not aware of Garrow's importance". In fact, Anderson was not to blame. In spite of Garrow's historical achievement, until recently his name has been little-known to lawyers or to members of the general public because he had been simply airbrushed out of history.

The question to be asked is, "Why?" Part of the answer lies in the fact that in one sense, he came from the wrong side of the tracks. Barristers and judges alike were products of the universities, often Oxford and Cambridge, and were supercilious towards a barrister whose father was a schoolmaster, who never went to university and who had been articled to William Southouse,[1] a solicitor in Milk Street, Cheapside. His graduate contemporaries venomously called him the "Billingsgate Boy" and treated him with contempt, even in the courtroom.

Nonetheless, he showed great ability in the law when working for Southouse and was encouraged to study for the Bar. He did so and was admitted by Lincoln's Inn on 27 November 1778.

---

1. It had been thought that the solicitor was a Thomas Southouse but diligent research by Ann Bremner of Wimbledon has established that he was in reality William Southouse. In the TV series he is called John!

Five years later, at the age of 23, he was called to the Bar. Then for ten years he was to outshine all those who had scorned him by bringing about outstanding changes in the criminal law that provided the inspiration for, and impetus to, the introduction of human rights for prisoners in England and across the globe.

Only now are his achievements being brought to light, after years of neglect. His return to prominence has much to do with the BBC series and to the first biography of Garrow, entitled *Sir William Garrow: His Life, Times and Fight for Justice*.[2] These have had the effect of bringing Garrow back from the far and dusty corner of the cellar of history. As a result there is now an irreversible change in the nature of discussions about the English method of criminal trial.

The Rights of Defendants

In an age when the rights of defendants were growing in importance, the focus of the criminal trial became, "the defence of the individual against the power of the state, rather than the state finding the offender on behalf of the victim".[3] As John M Beattie puts it in regard to Garrow, who exemplified the change,

> He placed a new emphasis on defendants' rights, indulged in aggressive behaviour, was insistent and pressing in cross-examining prosecution witnesses, challenged the rulings of the Bench, and his presence dominated in the courtroom.[4]

---

2. John Hostettler and Richard Braby (a direct descendant of Garrow), *Sir William Garrow: His Life, Times and Fight for Justice*, Hook, Hampshire: Waterside Press.

3. D Dwyer (2003), Review of John H. Langbein's *The Origins of Adversary Criminal Trial*, 66 *The Modern Law Review*, p.943.

4. J M Beattie (1991), "Scales of Justice: Defence Counsel and the English Criminal Trial in the Eighteenth and Nineteenth Centuries", *Law and*

Garrow's importance lies in the fact that he was the first to develop such techniques and skills and in doing so change the nature of the criminal trial.

"Old Bailey Hacks"

In Garrow's day, most barristers who practised at the Old Bailey, and there were only a few of them, were generally considered to be disreputable thugs and bullies. This may be another reason why Garrow did not receive the recognition due to him. According to Allyson May they were widely regarded, inside and outside the profession, as "Old Bailey hacks" and dishonest ruffians exercising low standards of advocacy.[5]

Calling for reform at the Old Bailey in 1834, *The Times* newspaper in an editorial complained of barristers there being "veteran brawlers and bullies" who were "irritable and foul-mouthed". For good measure the paper added that,

> The Old Bailey has long been a scandal to the country and a by-word expressive of everything coarse and indecent in the business of advocacy.[6]

As there were so few defence lawyers at the Old Bailey this must, in the main, have meant prosecuting counsel.

In part, these low standards may have resulted from the fact that in felony trials counsel were not allowed to represent prisoners, apart from occasionally cross-examining prosecution witnesses.

History Review, University of Illinois Press, pp.238 and 247.
5. Allyson N. May. (2003), *The Bar and the Old Bailey, 1750–1850*. Chapel Hill and London: The University of North Carolina Press. p. 2.
6. *The Times*. (4 November 1834) p.2.

The unfortunate result of this conception of the role of Old Bailey barristers, however, was that no one noticed the significant changes that were being effected in the English criminal law by Garrow and one or two who followed his example.

Leading jurists ignored what was happening because they were too high and mighty to look carefully at the transformation that was taking place within the precincts of the Old Bailey they despised.

This poor image of the Old Bailey may well explain how eminent jurists such as Sir William Blackstone, Sir William Holdsworth, James Fitzjames Stephen, Leon Radzinowicz, James Bradley Thayer and others, together with members of the Bar, all failed to see the significance of Garrow or the birth of adversary trial and the rights for prisoners for which he was so largely responsible. Did they consider they should not dirty their fingers in examining what went on in what they considered this sordid court? If so, they betrayed their calling.

Only Stephen even mentioned the change towards adversary trial and he failed to see how it had arisen. In his *History of the Criminal Law of England*, he wrote:

> The *most remarkable change* into the practice of the courts [in the eighteenth century] was the process by which the old rule which deprived prisoners of the assistance of counsel in trials for felony was gradually relaxed. A practice sprung up, *the growth of which cannot now be traced*, by which counsel were allowed to do everything for prisoners accused of felony except addressing the jury for them.[7]

---

7. James Fitzjames Stephen (1883), *A History of the Criminal Law of England*, London: Macmillan, vol. I. p.424. Italics added by the author of this work.

Adversary Trial

Adversariality was a process that revolutionised the criminal justice system, and saved the lives of countless prisoners. Significantly, it also swept across the world as far as the United States, where it was enthusiastically endorsed and accepted by Presidents Thomas Jefferson and John Adams, as well as in Canada to the west, and India, Australia and New Zealand to the east. And its progress still continues.

In the last decade a number of Latin American states have drawn up new criminal codes based on the adversary system of trial. Russia enacted an adversarial procedure code in 2001 and China is proceeding to a similar goal as are Georgia and the Ukraine. Similarly there are moves towards adversary trial in France, Spain, Italy and Germany. The impact of such developments is to create a global shift in criminal procedure and due process that makes universal human rights meaningful.

> In short, the common law trial became the crucible in which, for the first time in human history, a system was created for the practical and universal application of the doctrine of human rights.[8]

It is worthwhile, therefore, to examine the true nature of Garrow's gift to the world.

Why was the birth of adversary trial so important? In the first place prisoners were often illiterate and in ill-health and usually held in appalling conditions in prison before trial. Moreover, they and had no facilities to prepare a defence which, in any event, they

---

8. Richard Vogler (2005), *A World View of Criminal Justice*, Aldershot: Ashgate Publishing Limited, p.135.

were normally incapable of doing. According to Richard Vogler,

> It is not too much to see pre-trial incarceration (with the prisoner usually shackled in leg-irons up to the moment of arraignment) as a species of torture aimed at cowing the prisoner into passivity and submission.[9]

And once in the Old Bailey courtroom they had to fight for their lives before baying mobs and hostile judges with no defence counsel to help them.

They could not compel witnesses to attend court even if they could contact them and any who did appear were, like the defendant but unlike prosecution witnesses, not permitted to testify on oath — an important consideration at that time.

In contrast adversary trial was to enable prisoners to have an experienced advocate tackle the prosecution witnesses and, where justified, discredit their evidence. This developed into opposing counsel dominating the courtroom as against the earlier situation where the judge controlled the evidence of witnesses, and often the whole proceedings with an iron hand, frequently to the prejudice of defendants.

With adversary trial the judge became an umpire rather than a participant in the courtroom forensic battle. It also led, as we shall see, from the efforts primarily of Garrow, to the presumption of innocence and other rules of evidence which assisted prisoners.

---

9. Richard Vogler, *A World View of Criminal Justice, Op. cit*, p.134.

The "No-Counsel" Rule

It seems incredible today that prisoners could be denied the right to have counsel represent them. In order to understand the significance of the transformation to adversary trial it is necessary to appreciate that the "no-counsel" rule had existed for centuries.

From early times indictments for felony were taken in the name of the sovereign and it was considered *lèse majesté* for those indicted to be allowed counsel to act against the king or queen. This was laid down as a precedent by the judges in a case of rape in the reign of Edward 1 (1273-1307)[10] and it was to remain part of the law until the eighteenth century as far as felonies (i.e. most crimes) were concerned.

As we have seen, prisoners and their witnesses were also not permitted to give evidence on oath. This followed the precedent set by the ancient trial by ordeal, and meant that the result of a trial by jury was believed to bear a "divine imprimatur". Accordingly, a conflict of oaths between the parties was considered blasphemous and inappropriate. As a consequence only the prosecution, in the name of the monarch, could call upon witnesses to testify on oath which, at the time, greatly strengthened their credibility and the impact of their evidence.

The "no-counsel" rule had also applied for centuries to trials for treason. However, prior to the Glorious Revolution of 1689 Whig politicians and grandees had suffered persecution and the rule hit them hard when they were brought before the courts on trumped-up charges in treason trials. As a consequence, when they took power they introduced the Treason Trials Act of 1696.[11]

---

10. Year Books. 30 and 31. Edw. 1. (Rolls Series) pp.529-30.
11. 7 Will. 3. c. 3.

The 1696 Act gave prisoners on trial for treason the right to have counsel act for them in all respects. This was an important breach in the "no-counsel" rule but Parliament did not find it possible to recognise a similar right for the far larger number of prisoners charged with felony who had no aristocratic connections. The change for them was to come about piecemeal and largely as a result of what Garrow managed to do.

In felony trials the judges were slow to react but with the example of the 1696 statute before them they must have seen the injustice of the rule which meant the scales were weighed too heavily against prisoners charged with capital offences. And, with perjury by prosecutors endemic, one or two judges began to allow counsel into the courtroom, but only a few and only to cross-examine prosecution witnesses. Even in those few cases in the early eighteenth century, however, counsel were still not permitted the freedom they had been given in treason trials. They were not allowed to make a speech or address the jury, only cross-examine. This situation existed with very few barristers appearing for the defence at the Old Bailey until Garrow arrived in 1783 and dominated the court for ten years.

The Lawyers Capture the Courtroom

In that short period, although like everyone else he was unaware of the significance of what he was achieving, Garrow gave birth to adversary trial. This was his gift to the world. As a consequence the judges began to take a less pro-active part in criminal trials and began to act as umpires above the fray. Following Garrow's example the lawyers captured the courtroom. In doing so, they created a working culture of human rights which was swiftly given constitutional recognition in the United States Bill of Rights and the French Declaration of the Rights of Man. In a period of great change it was part of the eighteenth century Age of Enlightenment.

Indeed, the English model of criminal justice was adopted in the early stages of the French Revolution. It was only reversed by Napoleon in 1808 when he reintroduced the secret, authoritarian, inquisitorial system which for nearly two centuries has straddled across those parts of the world that were not influenced by the common law.

Torture and oppression have formed part of the history and structure of inquisitorial trial and this is preferred to adversary trial by dictators of all kinds. Hence, Stalin's Russia could boast in 1936 of its "democratic" constitution which in the absence of due process and adversary trial was drowned in the Great Terror of the same year in which millions of people lost their lives or were sent to the Gulag.

Rules of Criminal Evidence

(i) Presumption of Innocence

In England the criminal rules of evidence grew along with adversary trial and changes in trial procedure as defence lawyers grappled to secure maximum protection for their clients. The gradual recognition of the advantage to defendants of being represented by counsel was of great significance, heralding the beginning of the concept of prisoners' rights.

As part of this grew the idea, largely the creation of defence barristers, that prisoners were deemed to be innocent unless the prosecution proved their guilt beyond a reasonable doubt. As defence counsel became more involved in the courtroom the presumption of innocence and the beyond-reasonable-doubt standard began to be forcefully applied. In a trial in 1790, Garrow told the jury:

> Let the prisoner have the advantage of the doubt; it is better, as has often been said, that guilty men should escape from the difficulty of proof, and the doubt that hangs over that proof, than that you and the sacred administrators of justice sitting on this bench, should run the risk of dooming to death a fellow creature on precarious or uncertain evidence.[12]

However, it was not until a year later, in 1791, that Garrow was the first counsel to express the presumption clearly in an English court. In the trial of George Dingler for murder, he told the judge that it should be "recollected by all the bystanders (for you do not require to be reminded of it), that every man is presumed to be innocent till proved guilty".[13]

Despite Garrow's sweetener to the judge the judiciary was not yet bound to accept the principle although one or two judges led the way.

(ii) The Hearsay Rule

Prior to the 1730s, although hearsay evidence, i.e. out of court statements as a form of proof, was always unpopular there had been little restriction upon its introduction in criminal trials.

It was once barristers began appearing for prisoners that the dangers of hearsay were fully appreciated since it precluded cross-examination, the only function permitted to defence counsel in an effort to secure a not guilty verdict. Although the rule was not fully accepted by the judges until the nineteenth century it was sometimes

---

12. OBP Online. (www.oldbaileyonline.org) 8 December 1790. Trial of George Platt and Philip Roberts. Ref: t17901208-35.
13. *Ibid.* 14 September 1791. Trial of George Dingler for murder. Ref:t17910914-1.

adopted earlier and Garrow invoked it frequently.

With serious consequences, often death, flowing from a criminal conviction it takes little imagination to see the dangers in so-called "second-hand evidence". Repeating what another person has said may involve changes of emphasis or intended meaning or even miscomprehension of what was expressed. An example case involving Garrow's objection to hearsay was that of William Jones who was charged on 10 December 1783 with receiving stolen goods.[14] Here, a Mr Isaacs said he saw a quantity of locks and asked Mrs Dunn who they belonged to.

When, Garrow acting for Jones, told him he must not tell the court what she said, counsel for the prosecution, John Silvester, intervened to say, "He must tell his story". Garrow appealed to the court and was upheld by Mr Baron Hotham who appears to have been one of the judges who viewed evidential rules with some favour.

(iii) Self-Incrimination

The essence of the self-incrimination rule is that neither a prisoner nor a witness should be required to accuse himself, or herself, of a crime. This also grew into a principle when defence counsel began to appear in criminal trials although, ironically, sometimes as a protection against an aggressive cross-examination.

In a trial in 1784 where Garrow was defence counsel, he asked a prosecution witness, "How long at times have you been a smuggler"? Opposing counsel, John Silvester, objected saying, "That is certainly an improper question" to which Garrow responded, "He has told us already that he is a smuggler".

---

14. *Ibid.* 10 December 1783. Trial of William Jones for Theft. Ref: t17831210-105.

The judge then pointed out that, "If he was asked as to any act of smuggling, the question would be contrary to law". In other words the manner in which Garrow posed his question was in order.[15]

Nevertheless, several times in the next few years Garrow had to be restrained by judges from aggressive cross-examination likely to lead a witness into self-incrimination. This was one evidential rule that defence counsel were often endeavouring to circumvent.

(iv) Involuntary Confessions

In the early eighteenth century a confession was allowed to be given in evidence against the party who had made it. An example was the case of Margaret Wilson at the Old Bailey in 1722 when her confession was admitted despite her claiming at her trial that the prosecutor told her that if she would confess they would forgive her. Later that would have been treated as an inducement that would make the confession inadmissible.

In the years following Wilson's trial, the rulings of the judges differed one from another. Then, on 9 January 1788, Samuel Chesum was indicted for stealing an iron chain valued at £1 from Archibald Campbell. After the theft a witness, Joseph Kirkman, had taken hold of the young prisoner and told him that if he told the truth he would be as favourable to him as possible and Chesum then confessed. Prosecuting counsel argued that no promise had been made that would induce a person to admit to a crime of which he was not guilty.

Appearing for the prisoner and addressing the court at some length, Garrow's central point was that the principle was that if anything operated by threat, menace or promise to induce a party

---

15. *Ibid.* 26 May 1784. Trial of Joseph Dunbar for Forgery. Ref: t17840526-132.

to accuse himself or herself the confession would be excluded in favour of liberty and life. The judge, the Lord Chief Baron, agreed and the confession was excluded.[16]

Garrow, and other defence counsel, constantly raised issues of evidential rules many of which, in the words of J M Beattie, were referred by the court to the "judges in their post-circuit meetings at Serjeant's Inn" which helped to form "what amounted to a law of evidence in criminal trials". He adds that, "In 1700 there were few treatises on this subject; by the early nineteenth century there was a substantial literature, a market having formed among lawyers at the criminal bar".[17]

---

16. *Ibid.* 9 January 1788. Trial of Samuel Chesum. Ref: t17880109-38.
17. J M Beattie. (1991), "Scales of Justice: Defence Counsel and the English Criminal Trial in the Eighteenth and Nineteenth Centuries", 9(2) *Law and History Review*, Illinois: University of Illinois Press, p.233.

Chapter 2

Eighteenth Century London Life

Teeming Population

Trials at the Old Bailey in the eighteenth century gave a flavour of the colourful and vibrant life in the city of London, then the largest city in Europe. London had a population of some one million men, women and children and was a vast trading hub for most of the world. Its teeming population was made up of people who were generally poor and many of whom committed crimes to obtain money or goods of which they felt themselves to be—or were—deprived.

Poverty and typhoid were endemic. Sewers were just storm-water drains. A few houses had cesspits, from others sewage was thrown out of the window into open drains that ran down the middle of the streets.

Boys still had to climb up inside chimneys often at risk to their lives while washerwomen and coalheavers broke their backs for pitiable wages. Robbery, often with violence, was rife as was pickpocketing. Indeed, the so-called "Sir John" Pagan, a successful Chick Lane pickpocket, maintained a "warehouse" for stolen watches which he conveyed to Holland for sale.[1]

As one eminent lawyer and writer has observed:

> It was a London that comes down to us now in the painting of Hogarth, and in the poetry of William Blake who had the moral vision to see the tears of the chimney sweeps and to hear the curses of the city harlots, and to feel the cruelty done to children in the Poor House. Electorates were all gerrymandered, power was in the hand of corrupt politicians and court favourites, and there were 50,000 prostitutes living among the million people in London, not to mention such colourful characters as mudlarks, scuffle hunters, bludgeon men, Morocco men, flash coachmen, grubbers, bear-baiters and strolling minstrels. Wealth, of course, was all inherited: you were born into a certain rank and station in life and you were expected to stay in it … So when born in poverty you stayed in poverty, making ends meet by snapping up the gentry's unconsidered trifles.[2]

Absence of a Police Force

Despite the wealth concentrated in the West End the poor lived in insalubrious and crime-ridden areas. There was no police force and, as in the next century, there were "criminal districts in the metropolis, hot beds of particular crimes … a school for coiners, another for burglars, another for shoplifting, another for horse stealing".[3]

---

1. Peter Linebaugh (1993), *The London Hanged: Crime and Civil Society in the Eighteenth Century,* London, Penguin Books. p.225.
2. Geoffrey Robertson, QC (2010), Foreword in John Hostettler and Richard Braby, *Sir William Garrow: His Life, Times and Fight for Justice,* Hook, Hampshire: Waterside Press, p. xiv.
3. Liza Pickard (2005), *Victorian London: The Life of a City 1840-1870,* Weidenfeld & Nicolson: London, p.61. Citing Gustave Doré and Blanchard Gerrold (1872), *London*: London.

Some criminals were arrested, sent for trial and, if found guilty, executed or transported. Yet, at the same time, many innocent people were brought before the criminal courts where all aspects of everyday life were open for all to see. As the alleged felons pass before us in the Old Bailey trials, we can feel their poverty and helplessness whether they were charged with minor misdeeds or offences such as murder and robbery since most crimes were capital. And this feeling comes across powerfully in "Garrow's Law".

As we have seen, for centuries prior to the 1730s prisoners charged with felony were denied the right to have counsel defend them at all, even though they faced the gallows if found guilty. This applied to serious offences such as murder but also to trivial offences such as stealing a silk handkerchief worth twelve pence.

Prisoners were often thrust into court unfettered, ill and suffering from the hardships of incarceration in prison. And once there, they were told that without legal help they must provide a defence and prove their innocence themselves.

Yet the government paid large sums of blood money to bounty hunters when their allegations against people secured a conviction. This practice led to widespread perjury and the imprisonment or death of many innocent victims. Garrow attacked these so-called "thief-takers" ferociously to the delight of juries. Another difficulty for prisoners before Garrow was that criminal rules of evidence, such as the presumption of innocence, were unknown. Indeed, as shown earlier, it was in 1791 that Garrow was the first counsel to use the expression in an English court.

Felonies

Details of some of the offences tried at the Old Bailey are set out in the *Glossary* at the end of the book. The most frequent sentences handed down after guilty verdicts were the gallows or transportation. At that time many goods which are mass produced and cheap today were made by hand and were expensive to buy. These included handkerchiefs, clothing, pots and pans, goods made of wood, pins and needles, calico, rope, spoons and forks, all of which were frequently stolen and easily sold.

Despite the severity of the sentences for felony, including even fairly trivial theft, large numbers of people were charged at Assize courts with offences which today would be dealt with more leniently in the magistrates' courts.

To avoid charges of theft there seems to have been an informal custom among employees of taking "sweepings". This meant taking goods which had fallen to the floor or something similar. Workers believed they were entitled to them and they included coal, timber, coffee, beer and many other items including occasionally, gold. Sometimes employers—and juries–were amenable to the practice.

For instance, Robert Dixon, a journeyman printer indicted for stealing a book from a Strand bookseller, was acquitted by a jury who understood that,

> ... a practice ... prevails among compositors and pressmen of retaining a copy of every book they work upon.[4]

However, the jury appear to have ignored that the book was stolen from a shop and not picked up at the workplace. Two plumbers charged by the churchwardens of St Sepulchre's for stealing lead from the roof they were repairing were acquitted on the grounds of "it being customary in the trade for them to take such lead at a

---

4. *The Observer* newspaper (25 September 1796).

reduced price".[5]

Employers did not always agree, however. Mary Cheeseman was a servant of Rosemary Lane, a shoemaker who accused her of theft of children's shoes. Cheeseman claimed they were a gift but she was found guilty and transported for seven years.[6] James Tingay was a labourer who worked at a needle producing shop. He swept up and took 3,000 needles and was prosecuted and found guilty of theft.[7] Very likely he took too many!

However, although the gallows faced almost everyone convicted of felony, including for many different types of theft, the law was not so severe in practice as would appear from a perusal of the Statute Book. Against the severity of sentences must be set the exercise of discretion that was available during criminal proceedings.[8] The trial jury would often acquit an accused person for a theft from his or her place of work on the ground that there was a custom in the trade to do so. And, frequently they would deliver a partial verdict by reducing the value of goods stolen to make the offence non-capital. This practice is shown "Garrow's Law" and I will have more to say about it later.

The Old Bailey

The Old Bailey was the Assize court for London and, in addition to High Court judges, leading officials of the city sat there following the grant to the City of London by King Henry I of a degree of

---

5. *Ibid* (15 January 1797)..
6. Peter Linebaugh, *The London Hanged: Crime and Civil Society in the Eighteenth Century. Op. cit.* p.406.
7. *Ibid.*
8. Peter King (2000), *Crime, Justice and Discretion in England, 1736-1753*, Oxford: Oxford University Press.

control over criminal jurisdiction within its boundaries. The court dealt with felonies committed in both the county of Middlesex and the City of London. The trials held there that are reported in the Old Bailey Sessions Papers[9] reveal a great deal about the murky and criminal life of the time when a great deal of petty crime was dealt with at Assizes and the Old Bailey in addition to serious felonies such as highway robbery, rape and murder.

Trial procedure of the time would be unrecognisable today. Criminal trials were quick, prisoners were rarely assisted by counsel and the jury would not retire but huddle together in the jury box to reach their verdict. During the trial the jury and spectators would join in with comments, shouting, loud laughter and groans. The atmosphere resembled a bear-garden and this is well drawn in the courtroom scenes in "Garrow's Law".

Benefit of Clergy

For those found guilty, they might claim benefit of clergy for a first offence and be branded with a hot iron instead of being executed. Benefit of clergy was a hangover from the Middle Ages. It was concocted by the Church in the reign of Henry II and ensured that a convicted prisoner would be set free from the jurisdiction of the lay courts if he or she could read the first verse of psalm 51 (the so-called "neck verse"). This reads,

> Have mercy on me, O God according to thy loving kindness; according to the multitude of thy tender mercies, blot out my transgressions.

---

9. *Old Bailey Proceedings Online.*

Garrow invoked the benefit on a number of occasions and it was even known for judges to send a prisoner who had been found guilty back to the cells to learn the verse before returning to the courts to be set free.

Alternatively, those found guilty but unable to avail themselves of the neck verse might receive a royal pardon which would substitute a lesser punishment of transportation or set them free. These means of mitigating harsh punishments were quite widespread and, indeed, had to be so, otherwise the numbers hanged would have been so numerous "as to create public revulsion and destroy any legitimacy the law possessed".[10] The benefit of clergy was abolished by statute in 1827.

Coachmaker's Hall

Outside of the courtroom Garrow was a shy, retiring man. But in those days a young man could perfect his power of public speaking in the debating societies that proliferated in London. This talent was vulgarly called "spouting" but in more polite society it was known as the art of oratory. The environment was severe with interruptions, misrepresentations and derision from the audience that far overstepped the bounds of peaceful decorum. But this was only the rough exercise by which the speaker could learn to turn these obstacles to his advantage, and to display his courage and vigour.

Although he had a powerful and melodious voice it was not easy for Garrow at first as is shown by a reprint in *The Times* of Saturday 7 November 1840 of an earlier memoir of him in the monthly *Law Magazine*. This claimed that when he went with friends to the

---

10. Alison N May. (2003), *The Bar and the Old Bailey, 1750-1850*, Chapel Hill, University of North Carolina Press. p.14.

Coachmaker's Hall in Foster Lane, Cheapside in order to learn the art of oratory his timidity was such that they had to force him from his seat and hold him while he delivered his maiden speech lest he should shrink back from the task he had undertaken.

Nevertheless, battling to overcome his shyness he soon acquired a formidable reputation in the taverns as a speaker and was referred to in the press as "Counsellor Garrow, the famous orator of Coachmaker's Hall". By these means Garrow prepared himself for his role as counsel at the Old Bailey.

Advocate

William Garrow was called to the Bar by Lincoln's Inn on 26 November 1783 and made his mark immediately. He was never an accomplished academic legal scholar but instead became highly skilled as an outstanding advocate in the criminal courts.

For the whole period from the 1730s until the early 1780s Peter King has shown that defence counsel were involved in only some ten per cent of London cases. After 1780 between a quarter and a third of prisoners had counsel,[11] although barristers were still fettered within their restricted role. Garrow became the most experienced of Old Bailey advocates, as is clear from "Garrow's Law", and in some ten years he appeared in more than 961 trials there, in three quarters of them for the defence. In the year 1786 alone he acted in 117 of the 182 trials in which counsel were named in the Old Bailey Proceedings Reports. It is a remarkable record and he was probably involved in even more cases.

Miscarriages of justice were so common that the "no-counsel" rule

---

11. Peter King, *Crime, Justice and Discretion in England, 1740-1820*, Op. cit. p.228.

was being slightly relaxed when Garrow burst upon the scene at the Old Bailey in 1783 and entirely transformed the situation. Garrow was a consummate advocate, unrivalled in the art of cross-examination. But he was much more than that. Forbidden by the rules of procedure to address the jury, he framed his questions to prosecution witnesses as statements the jury could follow to the rage of prosecutors. He was an underdog acting for underdogs and he insisted on seeing his clients in jail before trial which was something else not permitted earlier. He mixed with and understood the criminals of the day and many learned to both fear and respect him.

On one occasion his wife, Sarah, was travelling with her granddaughter by coach from Ramsgate to London. Highwaymen stopped the coach and robbed everyone in it of all their valuables. The coach then proceeded along the road and the same highwaymen stopped the coach again. This time they gave back to Sarah all the articles they had stolen from her, and the little necklace taken from her granddaughter, keeping back all they had stolen from the other passengers in the coach!

The reported trials show, as does "Garrow's Law", how frequently he went beyond what was permitted for counsel and can truly be said to be the father of adversary trial and some of the rules of criminal evidence. But let us now look at the three series of "Garrow's Law" more closely to see how far they portray the astonishing scenes at the Old Bailey that bore Garrow's hallmark.

Part 2

Reality and Dramatic Invention

Chapter 3

"Garrow's Law"

BBC1

The television programmes on prime-time BBC1 were broadcast in 12 parts divided into three series. They were shown in the early winters of the years 2009, 2010 and 2011. The eye-catching picture they presented was remarkably true to the law and life in England in the 18th century. But to create dramatic tension Garrow's cases were sometimes changed in emphasis.

On occasion in state trials in which Thomas Erskine in fact acted for the defence (with Garrow, having left the Old Bailey to become a prosecution officer of the crown), Garrow is portrayed as defending, to reveal what was in essence the theatre that unfolded at the Old Bailey and in the High Court at the time.

A sub-plot running throughout the series is the relationship between Garrow and Lady Sarah Dore which adds a love interest and a poignant mother-and-child setting. This was largely fictional as in reality very little is known about Sarah and her relationship with Garrow other than it existed and eventually ended in their marriage. However, the sub-plot considerably strengthens the series and exposes the cruel and subjugated legal position of women in the society of the time.

TV Series 1

The first episode of series 1 starts with Garrow at the Old Bailey alongside William Southouse the solicitor to whom he had been articled. He is now a barrister after being encouraged to study for the Bar and having been called by Lincoln's Inn.

Seeing Eliza Radnell found guilty of stealing clothing worth more than one shilling and sentenced to death following a very brief consideration by the jury he expresses his disgust to Southouse that she was allowed no counsel for her defence. That is the first expression in the series of this major flaw in the criminal law that could cause injustice with dire consequences.

Garrow's First Case

In the second trial, based upon a real case, a man named Peter Pace is charged with highway robbery from a William Grove. In fact, he is innocent of the charge but has been arrested by a thief-taker named Forrester and taken before a magistrate on a trumped-up charge.

Thief-takers were common at the time and if the person they charged was found guilty they received a government reward of £40 — quite a large sum in those days. Of course, this led to both abuses and to perjury.

In the television account, this is Garrow's first case and it contributes to his education about the law and justice. Southouse tells him that he should not be too confident about success since Forrester is an experienced Old Bailey witness and he, Garrow, is not permitted to see the indictment against the prisoner, or the depositions taken at the magistrate's court before the trial.

Furthermore, he is not allowed to see his client in Newgate Prison nor can he address the jury. He can cross-examine prosecution witnesses and call his own witnesses as to the character of the accused but they cannot be *subpoenaed* to appear. Thus are all the cards stacked against the accused and his or her counsel.

The courtroom scene in the programme is entirely accurate and shows the court to be close to upheaval much of the time with considerable noise from the jury and spectators. Then there is an usher walking around the courtroom spraying it with incense to ward off the contagious pestilence of typhus known as gaol fever that frequently spread to the court from the adjacent Newgate prison. This fever was prevalent at the time.

Indeed, at the so-called "Black Sessions" at the Old Bailey in 1750 it killed four of the six judges, three counsel, an under sheriff and several jurors and spectators who all died of typhus contracted in court. According to Lionel W Fox, it was computed that every year a quarter of all prisoners were destroyed by gaol fever.[1]

In the TV trial John Silvester is counsel for the prosecution and constantly insults Garrow. He asks Garrow where he is from since, he says, he would know him had he been at Oxford. On learning that Garrow had been articled to Southouse in Milk Street, Cheapside he immediately calls him a "Billingsgate Boy" and, in the presence of the jury and the spectators, he tells the judge that this is Garrow's first case as a barrister.

In court William Grove identifies Peter Pace as the man who attacked and robbed him of two shillings—a capital offence. Garrow cross-examines Grove who had testified in the magistrate's court

---

1. Lionel W Fox (1952), *The English Prison and Borstal System*, London: Routledge & Kegan Paul Ltd, p.21.

that the attacker had his face covered.

How then asked Garrow could he identify the prisoner? By his horse, says the witness, and Garrow draws sympathy from the jury by asking if the horse is in the dock. But Grove also confirms that the prosecution is being paid for by Forrester who has much to gain financially if the case is successful. Forrester gives evidence and is also insulting to the new barrister Garrow in a manner that he was not so easily able to repeat in the future.

Garrow attempts to talk to the jury but is told by Mr Justice Buller not to make a speech. The jury find Pace guilty and, wearing a black cloth on his head the judge sentences him to death by hanging. Garrow makes some reference to being determined to see that criminal trials should become a contest with counsel appearing for the defence as well as for the prosecution — a forecast of what was to become adversary trial.

Infanticide

Elizabeth Jarvis is charged with the murder of her new-born baby. Lady Sarah, in the series the wife of Sir Arthur Hill, an extremely wealthy and prominent politician, attends the Old Bailey to take notes for her husband. She had earlier noticed Garrow and, feeling sympathy for Elizabeth, she tells Southouse that Garrow must defend her and she will pay.

There is no evidence for this in reality but it enables the BBC to introduce Lady Sarah and romance into Garrow's life. The important factor in this trial is that there is no presumption of innocence — that is to come later as a result of Garrow's efforts. At this time the onus is on the prisoner to prove her innocence. She has to show that the baby was born dead if she is to survive the trial.

Garrow desires to meet Elizabeth in Newgate Prison but is told by Southouse that he is not allowed to do so. He insists, however, so that he might explore all the possibilities in the case and not be faced by something unexpected in court. He gets his way and in her cell he asks Elizabeth why she denied that she was pregnant. She replies that had she admitted it she would have been dismissed from her employment without a reference and that she also felt degraded by her situation.

Garrow is determined to fight for justice this time and consults an obstetrician who describes the instrument for cutting the umbilical cord if it is tied around the baby's neck when born. A surgeon gives evidence for the prosecution and Garrow, using information gleaned from the obstetrician, is savage in his cross-examination to extract a confession from the surgeon that he is inexperienced in this type of case. At lunch, during an adjournment of the trial, Mr Justice Buller decries Garrow's determination and perceptively sees himself playing a lesser role in criminal trials in the future with the lawyers taking over the courtroom. This is precisely what eventually happened so that today the judge is an umpire and not an all-important participant.

On returning to the courtroom after lunch the judge admonishes Garrow for addressing the jury to which Garrow replies, "My Lord, I am only looking their way"!

Since he cannot present the defence case to the jury Garrow gets Elizabeth to tell them in emotional terms that the baby was not alive when born. However, the judge is determined that Elizabeth shall be found guilty and tells the jury that it is a clear case of murder. The jury, as was often the case in what was known as jury nullification, decides otherwise, however, and she is cleared with Garrow murmuring that he will change the nature of criminal trials for ever. In reality he was not aware of the revolutionary path he was embarking upon.

Duelling

In Episode 3 of this series, Garrow fights a duel with opposing barrister, John Silvester. Neither Richard Braby nor I have found any evidence that Garrow ever fought a duel but in "Garrow's Law" it is used to develop the relationship of Lady Sarah both with her husband and with Garrow.

In fact, in real life, when Hompesch, a Swiss nobleman and an officer in the British army, challenged Garrow to a duel Garrow declined to accept. The Baron had rented an estate in Kent and charged his neighbour, a farmer named Sherwood, with hunting game on his land with a dog. This was a violation of the game laws. Garrow defended farmer Sherwood, and in his defence he brought in the farmer's dog to establish that it was merely a sheep dog. In doing so he made fun of the Baron, stating that his cause was supported by two witnesses, the Baron and the dog, "of which the last was certainly an honest witness".

The Baron then wrote a letter to the Prince of Wales denouncing Garrow and saying that Garrow was, "henceforward unfit to be received in company of gentlemen".[2] But Garrow remained unfazed.

"Sweepings"

The next case in this series sees Garrow defending William Hayward, a coachman employed by William Champion Crespigny, a gentleman of Cavendish Square in the City of Westminster. Hayward is charged with stealing from his employer a chariot harness worth £10. The accused does not speak on his own behalf or call

---

2. J M Beattie (1991), "Garrow for the Defence", *History Today*, History Today Ltd, p.53.

witnesses and the defence rests entirely on the skills of Garrow who is persistent, and at times threatening, in his cross-examination of Crespigny and other prosecution witnesses.

Hayward's defence is that he had been given certain perquisites such as boots, breeches and the harness to make up his wages, somewhat along the lines of the "sweepings" referred to earlier. As Garrow draws out, Hayward had openly disclosed his ownership of the harness by displaying it for sale. At one point a prosecution witness, Sarah Pitt, endeavours to introduce something that Mrs Crespigny had told her but Garrow quickly points out that such testimony is hearsay and inadmissible.

Confident of his powers with the jury, Garrow declares, "I shall call no witnesses in such a case; and I advise the coachman to say nothing". The last conforming to what often happened at the Old Bailey. When the trial ends the judge tells the jury that servants have no right to "lay hold of the property of their masters and keep it as wages" but the jury finds the prisoner not guilty.

London's Monster

Renwick Williams was accused of being the monster who was roaming the streets of London and cutting the clothing of passing women. As this frequently involved some cuts to parts of the body of the women the monster's actions caused considerable public outrage. Garrow was instructed by Williams in a trial in which the prosecutor was Ann Porter. By this time Garrow had now established that he could visit any client in prison but the significant point in the trial, in which Porter was likely to succeed was, as we shall see, the point of law raised by Garrow. It was generally felt at the time that whilst Garrow was a good cross-examiner he had little knowledge of the law.

Brougham, for example, praised Garrow's courtroom skills but also said that there had "probably been few more ignorant men in the profession than this celebrated leader. To law, or anything like law", he said,

> ... he made no pretence ... and yet one important branch of knowledge had become familiar to him – his intercourse with prisoners, with juries, above all with witnesses, had given him extensive knowledge of human nature – though not certainly in its higher, more refined, or even more respectable forms.[3]

The "Billingsgate Boy" jibe again.[4] It is possible that Garrow had not the knowledge of law possessed by a graduate of Oxford but evidence in the Lincoln's Inn Library reveals that he took the study of criminal law seriously. Whilst a pupil barrister of Richard Crompton, Garrow industriously notated his copy of the 1677 edition of Euer's *Doctrina Placitandi* a book in two volumes on the Law of Pleading written in law French.[5]

In the 18th century to cut cloth was a felony for which the penalty was death. In the "Monster" trial Garrow produces a statute of 1721 which provided that the only penalty for cutting flesh was the pillory. He thereupon persuades a prosecution witness to agree that in the attacks on women clothing was cut only to get at flesh. Garrow has understood the law but the judge is determined to obtain a verdict of guilty and tells the jury so to decide. The jury, however, finds the

---

3. Lord Brougham (1844-5), "Memoir of Mr Baron Garrow", *Law Review*, pp.318-28.
4. But see the case of Merryman and Pickering referred to in the text.
5. Subtitled *Ou L'Art & Science De Bon Pleading* (1677), London, R & E Atkins. Sampson Euer was a King's Serjeant. Examined by the author by kind permission of the Librarian of Lincoln's Inn Library.

prisoner innocent as indeed he was since the attacks had continued whilst he was in prison and the culprit was eventually caught. Despite the verdict of the jury the judge has decided to refer the case to the 12 judges of England (as an early form of appeal) but in the meantime Williams, who has not been released and is unaware that the true monster has been captured, commits suicide in prison.

Lady Sarah Dore

As mentioned above, throughout the series there is a sub plot involving Lady Sarah and her relationship with Arthur Hill who is presented as her husband. In reality, they were not married although they did live together and have a child called William Arthur. The programmes introduce the romantic interest as she did indeed leave Hill for Garrow who accepted her child by Hill. This was unusual at the time, although later they were married. However, in real life she left Hill for Garrow before he was practising at the Old Bailey.

The first child born to Sarah and Garrow, named David William, arrived on 15 April 1781 when Garrow was still studying law. Also contrary to the malicious attitude Hill shows during the series he supported his son by Lady Sarah throughout the son's life even though he was brought up by Lady Sarah and Garrow. That much is known but in real life little more is really known about their relationship. Nevertheless, the portrayal of the conflict between Hill and Lady Sarah, particularly over their infant son, although departing from the true history gives a tension to the story and uses artistic license throughout the series which is completely justified from a dramatic point of view.

Furthermore, dealing with the Hill, Sarah and Garrow relationship enables the authors to show in the later episodes the subservient role of women in the law and bring to light the terrible legal position of women at that time.

In the programmes, Hill dispossesses Lady Sarah by cutting her off financially. Under the law of the time women had no right to vote or hold public office. Moreover, on marriage, as Hill and Sarah were in the series, a woman's legal rights became totally vested in her husband. Her children, her property, indeed her way of life, were all under her husband's legal control. If she was separated from her husband he retained control of her children and all her possessions. Hence, in the programmes Hill was legally entitled to keep their child and sue for the return of her jewellery, as he constantly taunted her. Only at the end, in a compromise in which Hill seeks to ensure that his career does not end in ignominy, does Lady Sarah obtain custody of her baby, Samuel.

A Case of Rape

This episode sees Edgar Cole charged with the rape of his servant, Mary Tollin. There are several features worthy of note in considering the actual TV trial. In the first place, Lady Sarah, who is believed to have been a lady of high birth, sits on the Bench with Judge Buller. This was not uncommon at the time when prominent people often sat on the Bench and, of course, would not be averse to making comments to the judge about the case before him. In "Garrow's Law", Lady Sarah's husband and the Home Secretary would frequently sit with the judge on cases they considered important to them. This in no way deviates from the reality in Garrow's day.

Another feature is that Garrow is reluctant to defend Edgar Cole when all his sympathies lie with the young lady victim. But Southouse, who was instructing him, invoked the "cab-rank" rule whereby a barrister, something like a taxi driver, has to accept any brief to appear in a court in which he practises even if he wishes to avoid doing so. This is considered to be one of the golden rules of the Bar and, once established by Thomas Erskine in 1792, it has become today enshrined in paragraph 602 of the Code of Conduct of the English Bar.

In the trial of Edgar Cole the witness for the prosecution is Mary Tollin herself. She testifies that on a Thursday a few days after taking employment as a servant to Cole he had dragged her upstairs at his home, pushed her on the bed, and raped her. Afterwards he had calmly asked for tea and sugar. On the following Sunday she had run away.

Garrow cross-examines her gently but she admits that she has a "foul disease" which she believes she has caught from Cole. She denies having lain with any other person. But, asks Garrow, if she was raped on the Thursday why did she remain in the house until the following Sunday when she ran away with another servant, William Johnson? Replying to questions she says that Johnson was sacked on the Sunday for "drinking the gin". She admits she had taken a glass herself and then lay with him. Cole, who was a bumptious individual was found not guilty. When he boasts openly to Garrow of his successes with women, Garrow scorns him. This was one of the few defence cases that Garrow was not happy to win.

The next case in "Garrow's Law" is that of Eliza Radnell who is accused of stealing clothing valued at more than one shilling. She denies the charge but has no counsel and after the jury confers very briefly she is found guilty. Garrow remarks on the fact that she had no counsel and it strengthens him in his determination to fight for justice.

Thief-takers

Garrow's next case revolves around the use of thief-takers who bring out his most aggressive cross-examinations and gains him much sympathy from jurors. In the late seventeenth century there was no police force in England and the government had enacted statutes that created a rewards culture for bounty hunters. A statute in 1692 provided a bounty of £40 a head to thief-takers for the capture and conviction of highwaymen.[6] Two further Acts extended the scope to include convicted felons and an Act of 1778 gave the courts power to provide blood money whether there was a conviction or not.[7]

The trial that appears in "Garrow's Law" at this point involves highway robbery. In the process it draws the attention of viewers to a number of the flaws in the criminal law that Garrow is to tackle. In the first place he is not permitted to see in advance the indictment on the basis of which his clients are charged. Clearly a serious disadvantage to prisoners on trial for their lives particularly as if the indictment contained an error the case had to be abandoned.

Secondly, he is not allowed to see in advance the depositions of the evidence given by the prosecutor at the preliminary hearing before a magistrate. Furthermore, he is not permitted to see his client in prison before the trial, although by this time Garrow is ignoring this rule which had placed defence counsel in an invidious position. As we have seen he could not address the jury and although he could call witnesses to testify to his clients' character they did not have to attend court. All these restrictions are gradually to be broken down largely as a result of Garrow's efforts.

In the trial itself Garrow represents a young man and woman,

---

6. Leon Radzinowicz (1956), *A History of the Criminal Law. The Enforcement of the Law.* London, Stevens & Sons Ltd, vol. ii. p.57.
7. 18 Geo. III, c. 19, ss. 7-9.

Thomas Enoch and Phoebe Pugh, charged with robbery with violence. They enter a shop and steal from the owner, Katharine Stanton, a case of lace worth £50. They run off with in and in a nearby alleyway they give it to thief-taker, Edward Forrester, who has paid them 28 shillings to steal it. In the shop Mrs Stanton urges her grandson Dan to chase after the thieves.

He does so and when he enters the alleyway he sees Forrester with the box and attempts to take it from him. Forrester then clubs him to death. Speaking to the prisoners Enoch and Pugh, whom he agrees to represent, Garrow tells them that they face death by hanging. Admit the theft, he says, and as they had been offered 28 shillings for the lace he will endeavour to persuade the jury that the theft was for goods valued at less than 29 shillings which makes it cease to be a hanging offence.

In court Mrs Stanton says that she asked Forrester to recover her box of lace and agreed to pay him a reward of £80 in addition to his blood money. She also, with tears in her eyes, cries out her blame of the prisoners for the murder of her grandson and there is near pandemonium in court as the jury and the spectators shout at the prisoners.

There is the usual bear-garden atmosphere in the court encouraged by incense being thrown about to keep away the gaol fever. And at one point the judge tells Garrow once again not to make a speech with the jury in mind.

Edward Forrester, the thief-taker, then gives evidence and attempts to be arrogantly insulting to Garrow which brings laughter in court. In cross-examination he admits paying for the prosecution. Garrow points out he had taken £40 in blood money for this case in addition to the £80 reward offered by Mrs Stanton. Further, he had been paid a total of £220 in blood money in the past year, which he does not deny. He testifies on oath that he had entered the home of the prisoners and had found there the box of lace.

The next prosecution witness is Sam Steele, an accomplice of Forrester. Under skilful cross-examination by Garrow he is induced to say that Forrester had entered the prisoners' home with a large bag and implies that he had planted the box of lace.

As a consequence of Garrow's suggestion as to the value of the lace the jury reduce it and the prisoners are not sentenced to be hanged but to be transported. As to Forrester, he is charged with perjury and sentenced to be placed in the stocks for two hours. As was usual when a person was in the stocks plenty of people pelted him with tomatoes and rotten fruit. In addition, however, in this case Mrs Stanton pays Sam Steele to throw a rock at him which either kills him or seriously injures him. Which it was is not clear in the programme. The whole case is a clear example of the type of adversary trial that Garrow was gradually forging.

High Treason

Garrow is now involved to defend Joseph Hamer who has been in prison for many months in 1794 on suspicion of sedition and plotting an armed uprising against the king. This is based, in fact, the famous case of Thomas Hardy the shoemaker that had vast repercussions in undermining a "reign of terror" planned by the government and the subsequent destruction of 800 warrants of arrest that had been prepared.

In preparation for the trial, *habeas corpus* was summarily suspended. The Old Bailey was surrounded by barriers and troops to keep out the press of anxious people thronging the streets. From mouth to mouth passed the word of the date — the 5th November. A fateful date for England.

On this day in 1604, Parliament had been in danger from Guy

Fawkes and the Gunpowder Plot. On this day in 1688, William of Orange had landed at the small fishing village of Brixham to restore the liberties of England and the Protestant religion. Now, in 1794, these liberties were again in peril. It is ironic that the government of William Pitt fearing the spread to England of the French Terror should itself prepare its own reign of terror.[8]

In reality, Hardy was brilliantly defended by Thomas Erskine. Garrow, after leaving the Old Bailey and joining service for the crown, appeared in a minor role for the prosecution. Lady Sarah has a significant role in this episode of the TV series which could not have been possible in the Hardy case and although there are numerous differences between the real case and the drama the latter maintains the fighting spirit of Erskine's powerful defence of Hardy although replacing him with Garrow.

It should be said here that those involved in making the programmes themselves pointed out that they were not making a biographical documentary. They endeavoured to link the convenience of drama with real cases and events. They stressed that the cases were real even if they did not involve Garrow. It was necessary to compress and elide, make up scenes and dialogue, but all the trials were true in substance, if not in historical fact, in their detail. Artistic licence, they argued, is necessary but must be balanced with the truth.

In the Hamer case in "Garrow's Law" the prisoner tells Garrow that he wants an opportunity to speak in court. Garrow replies that if he does so he will put a noose around his neck. This was in keeping with the development of adversary trial where instead of the

---

8. For the "Reign of Terror" see J R Green (1874), *A Short History of the English People*, London, The Folio Society (1992), p. 818 and Lord John Campbell (1868), *Lives of the Chancellors*, vol. vi. p.460, London: John Murray.

defendant making an unsworn statement the barrister would take control of the defence within the limits the law allowed. And as this was a state trial for treason, Garrow would also have the unusual opportunity of addressing the jury directly.

In "Garrow's Law" Joseph's wife Mary and his friend, Charles Lynam, are arrested at a meeting of the London Corresponding Society and Southouse secures their release in order that they may help prepare the defence.

Meanwhile, the Secretary of State, Viscount Melville, Sir Arthur Hill, who is MP for the rotten borough of Bramber in West Sussex, and a number of other MPs meet, and in fear of the French Revolution spreading to England, agree to charge Hamer with high treason. This was when they arranged the preparation of 800 warrants for the arrest of prominent people once Hamer, and two others who, in fact, were also discharged in their trials which followed, were found guilty.

The pompous Sir John Scott leads for the prosecution, assisted by John Silvester, and makes a very lengthy speech. He also reads from letters written about the holding of meetings and similar matters. These, interrupts Garrow, have no reference to the prisoner and are hearsay which should not be allowed. Silvester asks the judge for a ruling and he decides that they can be put before the jury. Garrow objects violently.

Despite the strained nature of Scott's speeches the case before Judge Buller proves weak. Accordingly, Sir John and Silvester offer Garrow a deal. If Hamer pleads guilty he and his fellow committee members will die but the offence alleged in the 800 warrants already drawn up will be reduced from treason to sedition. In the meantime, Melville's men plant and then find a receipt for one hundred muskets at Hamer's house.

Lady Sarah manages to get Sir Arthur to tell her about the plot against Hamer and she reveals to Garrow that Lynam is a government spy. When Lynam is in the witness box Garrow exposes him as the man who planted the bill of sale in his friend's house and informed the Secretary of State that it could be found there. This causes uproar in court with cries of "traitor" and "Judas".

Melville tries to influence Garrow by offering to raise him to the rank of King's Counsel. Garrow is tempted but declines the offer in a coded message in court to Melville who is sitting on the bench with the judge. Garrow then promises to give his version of the trial to court journalist Thomas Rawlings if he can find the names of the 800 men on the government's list of warrants.

Addressing the jury Garrow tells them that liberty of the individual cannot be taken away by government. Producing the list of names on the 800 warrants, which Rawlings has managed to obtain, Garrow tells the jury that all had been assumed guilty. Among the names, he declares, are some people in the public gallery. Some are lawyers including himself. One is a member of the jury. If they send Hamer to the gallows, Garrow foretells that the members of the jury may follow him tomorrow.

At the end of the trial Hamer is found not guilty to great acclamation in the courtroom and is discharged. The 800 warrants are then scrapped and franchise reformers could breathe again.

Although this was Erskine's case for the defence and not Garrow's the drama of the case is correctly portrayed and drawn to the attention of the television audience, which is what the writers desired.

Garrow and Erskine

Garrow and Erskine, although from very different backgrounds, had a great deal in common. They were contemporaries who often appeared in court in the same case—sometimes in harness and sometimes on opposite sides. There is evidence that they were friends. Both rose from rags to riches, earning huge fees and, more importantly, by sheer skill and eloquence they have to be regarded as two of the brightest stars ever to shine in English criminal trials.

It was perhaps because of their relatively lowly start in life that they both proved able to empathise with juries and somehow infuse their ideas into the minds of those 12 good men and true before whom they so frequently appeared. Erskine stood thin and erect, had a clear and melodic voice and a penetrating eye. Garrow could be more bruising in court and his questioning of hostile witnesses was more aggressive.

Garrow made his name, and introduced a culture of human rights into the criminal law, in the sordid atmosphere of the Old Bailey. Erskine too appeared at "The Bailey" but far less frequently, and he shone in the state trials that rocked England (and Scotland) when the government of William Pitt took fright at the idea that the French Revolution could spread across the channel.

We have seen with the case of Thomas Hardy, the shoemaker, how he succeeded in preventing an "English Terror". Lord John Russell wrote that,

> Defended by [Erskine] the government found in the meanest individual whom they attacked, the tongue of Cicero and the soul of Hampden, an invincible orator, and an undaunted patriot.

Garrow's impact in securing adversary trial had repercussions throughout the globe which are still with us today. And to his friend and colleague, Thomas, First Baron Erskine, goes the accolade of being the most outstanding advocate and champion of justice and liberty in English legal history.

Chapter 4

TV Series 2

Amicus Curiae

In the first brief case in the first episode of this series a young woman appears before the court charged with the theft of clothing, a sheet and a key. She is not represented and Garrow asks permission of the court to act for her as an *amicus curiae* (a friend of the court). The judge agrees and Garrow cross-examines the witness for the prosecution. How, asks Garrow holding up the key, does the witness identify the key as belonging to his mistress? Because it is rusty, comes the reply. Had the witness tried the key in a door? No.

The young woman herself then testifies that she had bought the clothes from a woman and that the key is the key to her own door. Garrow ridiculed the idea of the key being identified because it was rusty and says there is no prosecution evidence as to the door it fitted.

Lady Sarah then asks the indulgence of the court to speak for the girl and says she was a former housemaid of hers and she can give her a good character which she proceeds to do. The jury return a verdict of not guilty. Evidence of good character was always allowed at this time and such witnesses were often the only ones a defendant had.

The Zong Slave Ship

In this case the *Zong* was carrying 440 Africans to slavery in the West Indies. Fifty-four of them were women and children. It appeared that the captain had mistaken his bearings as a result of which the journey was taking far longer than it should have done. This enables him at some point to allege that there would not be enough fresh water for everyone before they reached their destination, some 300 miles away.

As he further alleges that the ship had become "foul and leaky", he decides to reduce the number of passengers. One hundred-and-thirty-three of the slaves are then thrown overboard while still alive. Whilst this murderous atrocity is being committed they are weighed down by irons. In fact, the insurance claim for the "lost" bodies was to exceed what the slaves would have fetched at the slave market.

To the defence suggestion at the trial of the captain that this was why the slaves were thrown overboard and murdered, John Silvester, for the prosecution, responds that in law the slaves are chattels and goods and not persons and thus could not be murdered. Questioned by Garrow, the first mate confirms the captain's statement that there was not enough water to go round.

The question before the court is whether the throwing overboard of some of the slaves was a necessity or was negligence. But the ship's log has been lost — itself a serious offence. Garrow, however, has the diary of a crew member named Robert Stubbs which was damaged by rain water.

Crucially, in the diary Stubbs had written that it had rained heavily prior to the disposal of the slaves and that enough water had been collected to satisfy everybody on board for the remainder of the journey. The judge accepts that and at the end of the trial the captain is found guilty by the jury. He is, however, sentenced by the judge to only two years in prison.

This was another case in which Garrow was not involved but the episode was based upon a true case and became part of the fabric of criminal trials at the Old Bailey that the writers endeavoured — successfully — to portray.

It was during this trial that Sir Arthur Hill accuses Lady Sarah of adultery with Garrow and claims that Garrow is the father of their child. He decides to cut her off financially and employs the services of a sinister attorney, John Farmer, to pursue Lady Sarah through the court of Doctors' Commons, the home of the ecclesiastical courts. As we have seen, in reality Lady Sarah was not married to Hill but they did have a child whom Garrow and Sarah later decided to bring up before they eventually married.

As we have seen, this in itself was unusual for the time and the conflict between Hill and Garrow formed a sub-plot for the series that added considerably to the drama.

Sodomy

In this episode on the television, Southouse takes his wife's shoes to be repaired so that he can talk to the cobbler, David Jasker, who has accused Captain Robert Jones of sodomy.[1] Jones claims he was being blackmailed, which was quite common with sodomy cases. Notwithstanding this allegation, in July 1772 he was convicted at the Old Bailey for sodomising a 12-year-old boy, Francis Henry Hay, and sentenced to death. He was, however, granted a royal pardon

---

1. For the full text of the trial of Jones see Rictor Norton, *Homosexuality in Eighteenth-Century England.* http://rictornorton.co.uk/eighteen/jones2.htm.

provided he left the country.

The pardon was granted on the ground that the boy had consented and had accepted a halfpenny on each occasion that the offence took place. The facts show that he was indeed seduced but seems calmly to have accepted the situation.

This was not a Garrow case and although such trials were not rare at the time reports of them were suppressed by order of the judge at the trial. Hence the Old Bailey Reports of this trial stick solely and briefly to the fact that the trial took place and not even a file number is given.

The Seamen's Hospital Case

Captain Baillie was a respected old salt who on his retirement from the sea had been appointed Lieutenant-Governor of the famous charity, Greenwich Hospital for Seamen. Here he uncovered serious corruption by the Admiralty in breach of the hospital's royal charter. Accordingly, in the TV series, on behalf of the men, he presents petitions to the directors of the hospital, to the governors and, ultimately to the Lords of the Admiralty asking for a full inquiry. Not one responds.

Without regard to the risk to himself he then publishes an exposure of the corruption involved, including the denial of food to the patients.

A graphic visual image is here portrayed showing the contrast between the foul food and drink given to the men in sordid surroundings whilst in a plush dining room the Admiralty men dine at a table replete with the finest food and wine that money can buy.

Lord Sandwich, who is First Lord of the Admiralty and who, for electioneering purposes, has improperly placed in the hospital a great many of his cronies from his country estate whom he makes freeholders to give them the right to vote.

The disreputable peer secures the suspension of Captain Baillie. Some of his placemen, who had never been to sea, despite the hospital charter providing that all officers employed at the hospital had to be seafaring men, then sue Baillie for defaming them.

Erskine's Guinea

Erskine, who defended the captain, received a guinea retainer in the trial of *Rex v. Baillie*. This was his very first case and his first guinea which he framed and kept as a souvenir. On the television Garrow, not Erskine, defends Baillie but the episode is true to the story of the trial. In real life the case came on for hearing in the King's Bench on 23 November 1778 with Lord Mansfield presiding. In the TV episode the prosecution allege that Baillie wants vengeance and is not concerned for the seamen. Garrow contends that Baillie has merely been doing his duty and that the men have been given horse meat to eat and watered beer to drink.

When, in reality, Erskine had attacked Sandwich, Lord Mansfield pointed out that the First Lord was not before the court. Erskine responded that he would drag before the court "this man who was the mover behind this dark scene of iniquity". Garrow does just that and follows Erskine's eloquence in the television trial in which he describes Sandwich as the sole ruler of the hospital. Although appointed by Baillie himself, as the fifth counsel for the defence Erskine was not expected to speak. However, he insisted, saying,

> I cannot relinquish the high privilege of defending [my client] – I will not give up even my small share of the honour of repelling and of exposing so odious a prosecution.

As on other occasions in the TV series, Garrow's questions to witnesses amount to his addressing the jury.

For the defence, he calls in aid a seaman who has been expelled from the hospital when ill with dire consequences not only for him but also for his sick wife and innocent children. So powerful is counsel's onslaught that it comes as no surprise that at the end of the trial Baillie is successful with the jury finding him not guilty.

Injustice for Children

The next case involves a young 12-year-old boy who is charged with theft from the Royal Mail. This is based on the real trial of Thomas Wiley, a 13-year-old, and, again, was not Garrow's case. In the television trial the prosecution witness, John Davis, sees the boy do something but the boy will not answer to him. This is not surprising since he is a deaf and dumb which was not true of Wiley and was a dramatic invention.

As commonly happened Garrow is told not to address the jury. There are no defence witnesses and the jury finds the boy guilty and he is sentenced to death. In the dock the boy presents a tragic figure. So young and with a faced marked by wide-eyed innocence he is bewildered by what he sees going on around him. When the judge passes the sentence of death with the black cloth on his head Garrow feels ill with disgust. It is, he declares, a barbarous punishment for a boy of 12. It seeps into his bones, he says, and is a "pantomime of justice".

Well might Garrow feel so since he often defended children and, appalling as this sentence was, it was by no means unusual at the time. For instance, on 2 August 1833 Lord Suffield introduced into the House of Lords a Bill to abolish the death penalty for simple housebreaking.[2] In the course of his speech he referred to a trial in the previous May of a boy named Nicholas White.[3]

Nicholas, aged only nine years, whilst playing with some other children, was tempted by them to push a stick through a cracked window and pull out some printers' colours. Despite the value of the colours being only two pence the boy was indicted at the Old Bailey for "feloniously breaking and entering a dwelling-house in Bethnal Green and therein stealing fifteen pieces of paint value 2d".

The young boy pleaded not guilty but was convicted and sentenced to be hanged under the Act Lord Suffield's Bill was intended to repeal.

It is noteworthy that in the Lords both Lord Wynford and the Duke of Wellington spoke against the Bill. Neither, however, cared to grapple with the facts produced by Suffield, nor did they venture to press the Lords to a division. In the event, the Bill received the royal assent 12 days later on 14 August—a remarkably speedy enactment.

Criminal Conversation

In "Garrow's Law", Arthur Hill (Viscount Fairford) prosecutes Garrow for criminal conversation with Lady Sarah and claims heavy damages. Of course, this did not happen in reality because Hill and Lady Sarah were not married. Criminal conversation was real enough though and was a polite term for adultery but with a special twist. It concerned equity, i.e. damage to the value of property, which was a theme of special interest in English law.

However, such cases were far from polite affairs. When a man had

---

2. *Hansard*, NS (1833), vol. 20. cols. 278-82.
3. OBP Online. (www.oldbaileyonline.org) (May 1833). Trial of Nicholas White. Ref: t18330516-5.

sexual intercourse with a married woman he could be sued for the financial loss sustained by the injured husband and for damages to the well-being of the husband's family since his wife was regarded in law as his property. For that reason she could not be called upon to give evidence.

A money value would also be set for "exemplary damage", a ruinous financial penalty intended to discourage potential adulterers from acting on their impulses.

On the television Hill engages Thomas Erskine to represent him and Garrow is surprised to find Silvester offers to act on his behalf which he does with sincerity despite his earlier disrespect towards Garrow. In the result the jury find for Hill but with damages of one shilling—a clear victory for Garrow.

At the time such cases involving high profile scandals were frequent in view of the very heavy damages usually awarded and in spite of the shock to society that was created by the reports. For an interesting real life case of criminal conversation in which Garrow, as counsel, was opposed by Henry Brougham there exists a 48-page book entitled *Crim Con!!, Damages Fifteen Thousand Pounds!* It was published immediately after the trial in which Lord Rosebery sued Sir Henry Mildmay for £30,000 in damages in 1814.[4] Garrow represented Lord Rosebery and extracts are given with comments in *Sir William Garrow: His Life, Times and Fight for Justice.*[5]

At one point in the trial Garrow told the court that Sir Henry Mildmay,

---

4. *Crim Con!! Damages Fifteen Thousand Pounds!* (1814). Case by Lord Rosebery Against Sir Henry Mildmay for Criminal Conversation with his Wife. London: John Fairburn.

5. John Hostettler and Richard Braby (2010), Hook, Hampshire: Waterside Press, pp.115-123.

> With the eloquence of a devil [...] urged her to cast off her husband, to abandon her duties as a mother and wife, and to sell herself to perdition.

Perhaps it is not surprising that at the end of the case the jury, after retiring for an hour and a half, returned a verdict for Lord Rosebery and awarded him damages of £15,000.

Chapter 5

TV Series 3

The Deranged Soldier

This was the trial of James Hadfield who, on 15 May 1800, fired a gunshot at King George III in the royal box at Drury Lane Theatre. It was another case where Thomas Erskine acted for the defendant and, in real life, Garrow acted as part of the prosecution team. Hadfield was arrested in the theatre and was subsequently charged in the High Court with high treason before Lord Kenyon and three other judges with a jury.[1] In the TV series the trial takes place at the Old Bailey before Judge Buller.

In opening the case for the prosecution in the High Court the Attorney-General, Sir John Mitford, told the jury that the facts would show that there could be no doubt of Hatfield's guilt unless the misfortune of insanity were offered as a defence.

In law, he continued, if a man's mind was so diseased that he was incapable of distinguishing between good and evil and was completely deranged then the mercy of the law held that he could not

---

1. *State Trials* (1821), xxvii.

be guilty of a crime. This was also stated as part of the defence by Garrow in the TV episode.

Both in reality and on the television the prosecution argued that Hadfield was sane although he had earlier attacked his baby, as a result of which his wife had left him. They called witnesses, including the Duke of York to whom Hadfield had served as an orderly, to testify to his sanity. Cross-examined the Duke said that when he spoke to Hadfield after the shooting Hadfield had told him he was tired of life and thought he would be executed if he made an attempt on the king's life.

Erskine argued (as did Garrow on the television) that delusion without frenzy or raving madness revealed the true character of madness for which a man standing for life or death for a crime should be acquitted. The accepted maxim of the law, he said, that every person who understood the difference between good and evil should be responsible for crimes was too general a mode of considering the matter.

Hadfield had been seriously injured in battle and part of his skull had been displaced and forced inward on the brain. By a second stroke of an enemy sword his brain had been cut open. As a consequence of these dire wounds, counsel continued, the prisoner imagined that he had constant intercourse with the Almighty, that the world was coming to an end, and like Christ he was to sacrifice himself for its salvation. That was the blessed sacrifice he imagined he went to the theatre to perform. It would be his inevitable execution for treason.

The judge indicated that he accepted that Hadfield was in a deranged state and asked whether the Attorney-General thought it necessary to proceed further. Sir John Mitford said he had no previous knowledge of the evidence given by the defence and agreed that the prisoner should be acquitted provided he was confined to a suitable place for the safety of society. Garrow, for the crown, asked if the jury could state in their verdict the grounds on which they based it; namely that they acquitted the prisoner for insanity at the time the act was committed. There would then be a legal reason for his future confinement.

Having been told by Lord Kenyon that if the scales of justice hung anything like even, it was their duty to throw in, "a certain proportion of mercy", the jury found the prisoner "Not guilty, being under the influence of insanity at the time the act was committed". Shortly afterwards a statute was enacted permitting detention during the pleasure of the crown of anyone acquitted of a felony or treason upon the ground of insanity.[2]

The importance of Hadfield's case was that counsel had circumvented the normal test of ability to distinguish right and wrong by arguing solely from the premise of Hadfield's clearly established delusion. Clearly, this was a significant case of the period that the BBC rightly thought would improve the public's knowledge of the law of the time. However, the case, and the ruling of Lord Kenyon, were not generally followed and in 1843 the waters were muddied by the *M'Naghten Rules*. These were laid down by the judges in response to questions put to them by the Law Lords following the shooting dead of Prime Minister, Spencer Perceval, by John Bellingham in the lobby of the House of Commons.

Briefly, the *M'Naghten Rules* returned to the test of ability to distinguish between right and wrong. This caused considerable confusion among lawyers until the enactment of the Homicide Act of 1957 which by section 2 provided that although irresistible impulse and mental disorder falling short of insanity are generally no defence to a charge of murder, a verdict of manslaughter must be

---

2. 40 Geo. III. c. 94. (1800).

returned if the accused was found to be suffering from diminished responsibility. This allows the judge a discretion as to punishment which, at present, is not available in cases of murder.

As for Hadfield, he was committed to Bedlam asylum, where the Duke of York visited him and where he outlived George III, and all the jurymen, judges and counsel involved in the trial. At the time of the trial he was only 29-years-old. When he had become a very old man, Lord John Campbell visited him and found him reading a newspaper and talking very rationally on the topics of the day. He concluded, however, that he continued to be subject to strong delusions at times and that it would be very unsafe to discharge him from custody.

Pious Perjury

In the second episode of Series 3 we first see a man sentenced to hang for stealing three candlesticks. Then comes a case of breaking looms and cutting silk in which Garrow acts without fee because he believes the men think they have a cause.

Garrow's aggressive style of cross-examination often uncovered circumstantial information that motivated juries to bend the rules and reduce the severity of punishment. In the major case in this episode two men, Quinn and Foley, are accused of destroying looms and cutting silk in a Spitalfields Mill as an act of industrial sabotage. Garrow acts without fee believing the men, who were members of an unlawful trade union, were sincerely acting in a cause in which they believed.

The main prosecution witness, Matthew Bambridge, is a thief-taker upon whom Garrow pours scorn to such effect that the judge tells the jury to beware of Garrow "playing them like a harpist". But Bambridge had not identified the two accused men for a month and then only after a reward was offered for naming the men involved. He alleges that Quinn had written an inflammatory leaflet but Garrow reveals that Quinn cannot read and that Bambridge knew of it since he had earlier signed for Bambridge a receipt for wages with a cross. This causes uproar in the court.

Foley is persuaded to turn King's Evidence and testifies that he took part in the offence as did Quinn. He does this to secure his own release and is told by Garrow, "You smell the gallows; you smell the rope".

When the jury bring in a verdict of not guilty in favour of Quinn, Judge Buller tells them to change their verdict—but they decline to do so, saying "it is our verdict", in a fine example of jury nullification.

Nullification occurs (as it still does on occasion) when a jury exercises its power to acquit a defendant on the basis of conscience even when, on the evidence and the law, the defendant is guilty. Pious perjury occurred when capital punishment existed for numerous property crimes, many of them minor. Juries frequently reduced the value of the property and thus lessened the sentence, often from death to transportation. This arose when the death penalty was considered to be too harsh and out of proportion to the offence. When this occurred the judge was powerless to interfere with the jury's verdict.

A frequent example arose when the jury reduced the value of goods stolen to below 12 pence—above which the defendant would face being sent to the gallows. This had the effect of making the criminal law of the time less harsh than was previously supposed. The term "pious perjury" was coined by Sir William Blackstone who wrote that "the mercy of juries often made them strain a point, and bring in larceny to be under the value of twelve pence when it was really of much greater value ... a kind of *pious perjury*".[3]

In the 18th century nullification and pious perjury were widespread. For instance, Peter King in the research for his *Illiterate Plebeians, Easily Misled* (1988) found that around one-seventh of those indicted for property crimes in the major courts of Essex between 1740 and 1805 had the indictments dismissed as "not found" by the grand jury. The actual (petty) jury trial then acquitted almost a third of the remainder and brought in pious perjury verdicts for a further ten per cent. These figures are highly significant and between 1782 and 1787 similar figures were to be found in the counties of Surrey, Hertfordshire, Kent and Sussex.[4]

Garrow approved and, as the law forbade him from addressing juries directly, he often indirectly encouraged them to engage in pious perjury. One such case occurred in 1784 when Garrow defended Elizabeth Jones and Mary Smith on charges of shoplifting goods valued at 14 shillings. A part of Garrow's cross-examination of the chief prosecution witness is to be found in the biography of Garrow[5]. There was too much evidence against the prisoners for them to be acquitted but by his cross-examination Garrow gave the jury an opportunity to indulge their inclinations by giving a partial verdict and they found the prisoners guilty of stealing fans worth 4s. 10d.

By putting the value of the stolen fans below five shillings the jury, in another example of pious perjury, prevented the women

---

3. Sir William Blackstone (1830),*Commentaries on the Law of England*, London: Thomas Tegg, vol.vi. p.248.

4. Peter King, "Illiterate Plebeians, Easily Misled: Jury Composition, Experience and Behaviour in Essex, 1735–1815". In Cockburn and Green (eds) (1988), *Twelve Good Men and True: The Criminal Trial Jury in England, 1200–1800*, New Jersey: Princeton University Press, pp.254-5.

5. John Hostettler and Richard Braby (2010), *Sir William Garrow: His Life, Times and Fight for Justice*, Hook, Hampshire: Waterside Press, pp.59-60.

from being sent to the gallows and they were each sentenced to be whipped and confined to hard labour for 12 months in a house of correction. Penalties that were outrageous enough by modern standards but far better than a painful execution by the hangman.

Another example is to be found in the trial of John Merryman and William Pickering an examination of which is to be found in the "Garrow's Trials" section of the Garrow Society website.[6] In this case the jury are seen to be asking the judge if they have the power to bring in a partial verdict. The jury had found the prisoners guilty of housebreaking and stealing goods to the value of 32 shillings—a capital offence. Garrow addressed the judge and pointed out that before the verdict was recorded it should be noted that as to the capital part of charge there was no evidence other than that of an accomplice. Without his evidence, although the house had been entered and a theft had taken place, there was no breaking and entering to make the case capital.

The jury said it was their wish to leave out the capital part but they had doubts about their power to do so. The judge confirmed that they had the power and Garrow urged them to alter their verdict as it had not yet been recorded. This the jury then did finding the prisoners guilty of theft of goods to a value of four shillings and ten pence and they were then sentenced to seven years' transportation.

Pro Bono Publico Work ("Work for the Public Good")

On the television, in one case Garrow is briefly presented as acting for the defence without fee. In reality this was by no means unusual. In a trial heard on 10 December 1783, two women, Sarah Slade and Mary Wood, were charged with stealing clothing from a dwelling

---

6. See garrowsociety.org

house but had no counsel to represent them. Garrow undertook to cross-examine the prosecution witnesses for them without fee.[7]

The defendants were arrested by an officer of justice who told the court that he recollected that they had been in his custody before. "You know you are not to tell us that", interrupted Garrow. "I am telling you the reasons why I stopped them", the officer replied.

When Garrow told him he was not to give his reasons he responded, "I am not talking to you, I am talking to my Lord". Garrow immediately appealed to the judge who accepted his argument and allowed the witness to say merely that he knew the women before.

After further evidence and some disputes between the witness and counsel the jury found the prisoners not guilty and they were released. They must have been profoundly delighted that Garrow had offered to help them although they were unable to pay his fee.

Garrow later served without fee for a Sarah Pearson who was indicted for the offence of returning to England from transportation without lawful cause.[8] She gave evidence that she had been taken illegally to Jamaica where she served for six years before she returned to England to seek a cure for her lame leg which prevented her from working. In response to a question from the judge, Mr Justice Grose, she said she had no witnesses. Garrow asked the court,

> My Lord, as this poor woman has no counsel, will you permit me as *Amicus Curiae* (a friend of the court) to ask John Owen (the prosecution witness) a question or two?

---

7. OBP Online (www.oldbaileyonline.org) 10 December 1783. Ref: t17831210-44.
8. OBP Online (www.oldbaileyonline.org) 24 February 1790. Ref: t17900224-75.

The judge agreed and in reply to Garrow's cross-examination Owen agreed that the prisoner was telling the truth. Garrow persuaded the jury who said, "We think she was not at large without lawful cause" and acquitted her.

Dispute with the Bench

In much of the TV series, it is noticeable that the judge is frequently favourably disposed towards Garrow. This is not clearly shown in the Old Bailey Reports, however, and there can be no doubt that in defence of his clients, and pressing forward the role of counsel for the defence, Garrow was prepared to do battle with the Bench.

A case in point is that of William Bartlett, charged with theft on 11 January 1786.[9] Here, Garrow objected to a prosecution witness, John Rasten, being sworn. He argued that as Rasten was deaf and dumb he could testify only through an interpreter, his wife, to whom Garrow also objected. Mrs Rasten claimed to be a satisfactory interpreter because, she said, she would look up to heaven to show her husband that he should answer seriously. The dispute between counsel and Mr Justice Heath then arose.

Garrow quoted from Sir Matthew Hale, a view totally unacceptable today, that a deaf mute was presumed to be an idiot and could not communicate with the court. The judge said he remembered a deaf and dumb man being sworn in the Court of Common Pleas and he accepted that sign language was sufficient, although Garrow continued to disagree. This led to the following exchange:

Heath: You must not interrupt, your objection is premature.

---

9. OBP Online (www.oldbaileyonline.org). 11 January 1786. Trial of William Bartlett. Refs. t17861130 and t17860111-1.

Garrow: My Lord, I was not objecting, I was going on with my Examination and your Lordship did me the honour to interrupt me.

Heath: You will examine your Witness with some degree of decency. Your conduct and behaviour are very improper. What you do here is by permission of the Court in a Criminal Case.

Garrow: My Lord, I object to the Witness being examined and I take the liberty to state my objection to the Court.

Heath: You must examine your Witness.

Garrow: I have a right to my Objection.

Heath: If you do not examine your Witness you shall sit down.

Garrow: My Lord, I shall not sit down.

Heath: Then I shall commit you.

Garrow: So your Lordship may.

Heath: Then I certainly will commit you.

Garrow: There is a point of Law to be argued.

Heath: There is no point of Law and if there was you are to be Assigned to the Court but you are to behave with decency.

Garrow: So I do my Lord. I have not been used to be interrupted. I am here to argue points of Law for the prisoner.

Heath: You have no right until you are Assigned.[10]

Garrow: If you tell me so my Lord, I sit down.

Not to be outdone, however, later in the trial, Garrow made a long speech to the judge in the hearing of the jury. He pointed out that even if the witness and the interpreter could converse that did not prove the witness was capable of understanding complex ideas, particularly the principles of the Christian religion that underlay the binding power of the oath.

He then added,

> My Lord, I wish I could also address the jury on this trial. I should be glad to ask them whether they should choose to convict a man of felony upon the testimony of a man with whom they could not hold a conversation.

Bearing in mind the presence of the jury, Garrow concluded with an apology for what might have been considered his earlier "intemperance or indecency", adding that by his zeal on behalf of his client he had intended no disrespect to the "great and brave and venerable and learned judges of the law of England". In the event, on the evidence of the witness Rasten, Bartlett was convicted and transported for seven years.

---

10. Prior to the Prisoners' Counsel Act 1836 defence counsel were not instructed by the prisoner to argue points of law but were assigned by the court. The point of law could be raised by the prisoner, the judge or any barrister in court. D J A Cairns (1998), *Advocacy and the Making of the Adversarial Criminal Trial. 1800-1865*, Oxford: The Clarendon Press. pp.46-7.

Torture in Trinidad — The Picton Trial

At this point the TV programme presents a case of torture in Trinidad. Garrow practised law in the criminal courts during that period of English history when the sugar planters of the West Indies held great power in Parliament. Their monopoly, and huge profits, were possible because of the slavery of Africans transported there with its various practices to keep the slaves subjugated and the plantations free from the disruptions of the ever present possibilities of rebellion.

Garrow's stand on this issue was clearly described in an article about him published in the *Monthly Law Magazine* and republished in *The Times* shortly after his death. It states:

> With all the zeal that he was ever ready to display in causes confided to him ... Garrow was never ready to undertake a case which would oblige him to profess, in a public manner, opinions which were repugnant to his principles. Thus, at an early period of his life, when the question concerning the manner in which Negroes were obtained, and conveyed from Africa to the West Indies, was in agitation, he had formed a most decided judgment on the facts and on the traffic.
>
> One day Mr Fuller, a great West India proprietor, meeting him in the street, said, Well, Mr Garrow, here is plenty of business, and plenty of money for you; the committee have determined to retain you, and give you the management of all their business in Parliament and elsewhere". He answered, "Sir, if your committee would give me their whole incomes, and all their estates, I would not be seen as the advocate of practices which I abhor, and a system which I detest".[11]

---

11. *The Times* (7 November 1840).

These deep feelings were given expression when, in real life on 24 February 1806, Garrow prosecuted General Thomas Picton for inflicting torture on a British subject without legal or moral authority. In the television series he defends the object of that torture, a young girl named Luisa Calderon on a charge of theft. Earlier, in Trinidad, she denied the charge and, as there was insufficient evidence against her, the Spanish magistrate, who felt he had insufficient power to secure a confession, appealed to General Picton, Governor of the island to supply the deficiency. Picton then wrote in his own hand, what Garrow was to describe as "this bloody sentence":

Inflict the torture upon Luisa Calderon.

Calderon was held in prison for eight months in fetters and torture was applied to her.

When Picton was transferred to England for trial, Garrow decided to expose the horrors of colonial rule and brought to light the many kinds of torture practised in the West Indies, often resulting in death. In the television we see his vivid and savage cross-examination of the arrogant Picton which results in the jury finding him guilty.

In real life, after he was found guilty Picton secured a motion for a new trial. After much debate in the new trial the judge ordered a recess and in the event the trial was never resumed. Picton's reputation was shattered and he did not dare to return to the West Indies. Instead, he joined the army of Wellington and fought at Waterloo where he died with a bullet in his head. Portrayed as a national hero, Picton's hat with a bullet hole near the junction of crown and brim is on display in the National History Museum at Sandhurst.

He is buried in the crypt at St Paul's Cathedral and there is a large statue of him in the north transept of that great cathedral. But the last word may remain with Wellington who said that Picton, though a fine soldier, was, "a rough, foul-mouthed devil as ever lived".[12]

Moral Issue of Slavery

Within a year of the Picton trials, Parliament passed the Slave Trade Abolition Act of 1807. However, the statute proved difficult to enforce whilst slave traders continued to enrich themselves from this trade in human beings. Consequently, the first conviction for evasion of the Act did not take place until as long as ten years after its enactment. And as he made clear to the House of Commons on 28 February 1817, Garrow, who was Attorney-General at the time and had strong views on the moral issue of slavery which he considered an odious and immoral evil, took pride in securing that conviction.[13]

All the available evidence points to the trial being that of John Bean Hannay which took place at the Old Bailey on 19 February 1817.[14] Hannay was charged with kidnapping slaves, men, women and children, and carrying them away from Calabar in what is now Nigeria with intent to sell them. A special jury, sitting with Mr Justice Holroyd, found Hannay guilty and he was sentenced to transportation for seven years.

Slavery itself was finally abolished in 1833 by the Slavery Emancipation Act at a cost of £20 million paid in compensation to slave owners.

---

12. Elizabeth Longford (1969-72), *Wellington: The Years of the Sword*, London: Weidenfeld & Nicolson.
13. R G Thorne (1986), *The History of Parliament: The House of Commons 1790-1820*, vol. iv. Member G-P. London: Secker & Warburg. p. 7. .
14. OBP Online (www.oldbaileyonline.org) 19 February 1817. Trial of John Bean Hannay. Ref:t8170219-123.

Death on the Hustings

The final trial in the television series was based upon a real trial in 1784 in which both Garrow and Erskine appeared for the defence. Patrick Nicholson was tried, with three other men, for murder during an election in the city of Westminster in which the candidates were the Whig leader, Charles James Fox, Lord Hood and Sir Cecil Wray.[15] In Parliamentary elections at the time, Westminster had one of the largest electorates in the country and the elections, which took place over several weeks, were frequently riotous. The hustings were held in the portico of St Paul's Church, Covent Garden.

On the occasion that led to the trial the local police were present but there was also a considerable force of constables brought in from Tower Hamlets in east London. One of them, Nicholas Casson, was clubbed down in a scuffle and died shortly afterwards from his injuries. On the television the prosecution allege Casson was killed by the defendants but they have difficulty in establishing who had hit him. Their problem is added to by the skilful cross-examination of witnesses by Garrow and Erskine.

The thrust of the prosecution case is that butchers armed with marrow-bones and cleavers had attacked the police, which is hotly denied by the defence, but their witnesses are able to say little as to the actual killing.

Defence witnesses swear they had seen a considerable body of constables, probably as many as one hundred, attack the crowd with long staves without provocation. The judge, Mr Baron Perryn, indicates to the jury that because of the contradictions on the part of the witnesses for the prosecution they have to determine whether they should not acquit the prisoners. This they duly proceed to do,

---

15. OBP Online (www.oldbaileyonline.org) 1 June 1784. Ref: t17840601-1.

giving an example of the powerful influence of counsel's cross-examination even without an opportunity to address the jury.

In the television adaptation, once this stage is reached the daughter of Casson, Emeline, approaches Garrow to act for her in investigating and prosecuting the man who really killed her father. Garrow does so and with the aid of a Mrs Jacob, traces a Richard Lucas on whom he exercises a citizen's arrest in a bar. Mrs Jacob gives evidence that she had seen Lucas, who could be identified by a scar on his face, strike Casson on the left side of his temple, a blow which caused his death.

Garrow sets out to prove that the treacherous Chief Constable Sir Sampson Wright gave the orders to the constables and is, therefore, an accomplice guilty of constructive murder. However, Lucas is then mysteriously killed in his cell and the trial, and the attempt to bring Wright to justice, are abandoned.

In this episode Lady Sarah has escaped with her baby son and with Garrow's help manages to provide Arthur Hill with evidence that Viscount Melville has defrauded the Treasury. This enables Hill to advance his career in exchange for which he agrees to stop pursuing Lady Sarah who becomes able to live openly with Garrow and her son, Samuel.

Chapter 6

Afterword

Coal Face of Legal History

Some of the trials dealt with by the BBC take place after Garrow had ceased to practice at the Old Bailey. In them he appeared for the crown as one of the prosecutors in state trials in which Erskine often appeared for the defence. Garrow had changed sides. He became an MP for a rotten borough and, in turn, Solicitor-General, Attorney-General and a judge. Like Erskine, who was far greater as an advocate than as a Member of Parliament or Lord Chancellor, Garrow was not distinguished in any of these later roles despite the fact that he continued to have a long and successful legal career.

After helping to give birth to adversary trial he remained deeply involved in the procedural system while it was being fully institutionalised in society. As a prosecutor he interacted with the defence counsel now coming forward and, as a judge in the criminal courts he managed this new arrangement with all the rules of the game he helped create. Hence, he was always involved from the near inception of the system until it was the basis on which the criminal courts functioned.

But nothing reduces the value of what his genius achieved at the Old Bailey In his Introduction to the biography of Garrow, the civil liberties and human rights lawyer, Geoffrey Robertson QC, writes:

> There is also, importantly I think, the fact that Garrow, after his incandescent first decade at the defence Bar, "went over to the dark side", became a reactionary Tory and conducted some of Pitt's paranoid prosecutions against radicals. They were defended by his friend and rival Lord Erskine, who became in consequence the man more celebrated. But our recent conversion to human rights brings Garrow – who did so much to kindle them at the coal face of legal history – back into focus.[1]

We do not know what made Garrow change. Perhaps he had a deep resentment at being treated as the "Billingsgate Boy" and wanted to prove himself equal to those who sneered at him. But whatever the reason we should always remember his unique contribution to the valuable procedure that allows the individual directly to challenge any allegation made by or on behalf of the state.

If we wish to see Garrow as the real person he was we should also remember his charity work including his role in supporting a range of social reforms to benefit the teeming poor in British society at the time. It appears he was a life member of the Philanthropic Society and an active Vice-President of the Royal Humane Society pioneering in the techniques and system for rescuing and resuscitating shipwrecked people and other drowning victims in need of emergency help to remain alive.[2] It may be that this interest arose

---

1. Geoffrey Robertson QC (2010), Foreword to John Hostettler and Richard Braby, *Sir William Garrow: His Life, Times and Fight for Justice,* Hook Hampshire: Waterside Press, p.xiii.

2. I am indebted for the information in this paragraph to Richard Braby who

from having a home on the cliff top at Pegwell Bay, Ramsgate.

He was also a Vice-President of the Royal Sea Bathing Infirmary near Margate which took poor children from the streets of London to their own special hospital at the coast to aid their recovery.

The BBC, and the writers of "Garrow's Law," are to be congratulated for helping to bring Garrow into the public eye in so successful a series of prime-time television programmes.

Both trial by jury and adversary trial are crucial in helping to preserve human rights and establishment efforts—and those of governments of both colours—to undermine them must be resisted to the utmost. It may well be that bringing Garrow and his achievements to life for millions of people will help to ensure that they are not tampered with.

---

has been in correspondence about Garrow with Muriel Whitten, whose book, *Nipping Crime in the Bud: How the Philanthropic Quest was Put Into Law* was published by Waterside Press in 2010.

Glossary 1

Judicial and Historical Terms in use in Garrow's Time

Adversary trial
A criminal trial in which there is a clash of proofs presented by the parties and their counsel. The decision is reached by an independent, randomly chosen, jury with a judge who sums up the evidence to the jury and rules on points of law but otherwise takes no part in the proceedings. It is often contrasted with the **inquisitorial system of trial** where the judge conducts both the ore-trial proceedings and the case in court.

Assizes
Originally regional criminal courts, including the Old Bailey, which dealt with indictable offences. They were abolished by the Courts Act 1971 and replaced by Crown Courts the following year.

Associations for the Prosecution of Felons
Voluntary societies whose members' contributions were used to pay the expenses of criminal investigations and fees to counsel for prosecutions. They also offered rewards for information and thereby

often induced perjury and false prosecutions by thief-takers and bounty hunters.

Attorney-General
The principal law officer of the Crown and head of the Bar. He or she is usually a member of the House of Commons and changes with the administration.

Benefit of clergy
Device concocted by the Church in the reign of Henry II whereby a convicted prisoner would be set free from the jurisdiction of the lay courts if he or she could read the first verse of psalm 51 (the so-called "neck verse"). The benefit was not available to women until 1624 and treason was never "clergyable". In Tudor times it was provided that the benefit could not be claimed more than once, leading to branding for the purpose of future identification. It was abolished by statute in 1827.

"Best evidence" rule
This provides that evidence must be original and not derivative and must have a clear connection with the fact to be proved. Under it **hearsay** was normally excluded once rules of evidence were established in the eighteenth century.

Capital crime
Offences punishable by death.

Common law
That part of the law formulated, developed and administered by the judges of the common law courts as distinct from statute law. It is not written down in any one place but survives in law reports.

Confession
An admission of guilt made by a person charged with a crime. It became inadmissible in the eighteenth century if made in response to an inducement or threat.

Cross-examination
The right of defence counsel to question prosecution witnesses. It is not confined to matters alleged in examination-in-chief and may include leading questions. Once permitted to counsel in the eighteenth century it made possible the development of adversary trial.

Dock
The box in which a prisoner stood in court.

Examination-in-chief
Oral examination by prosecuting counsel of his witnesses. It may not include leading questions. Similarly by defence counsel of defence witnesses.

Habeus Corpus
A prerogative writ used to produce before the courts persons detained illegally. It is Latin for "You have the body".

Hearsay
So called "second hand evidence". Statements made out of court and not subject to cross-examination. Generally permitted before the eighteenth century but subsequently disallowed after pressure for its exclusion by Garrow and other defence counsel.

Indictment
Formal written accusation charging one or more persons with a

felony and reciting the charges in technical language. If the accused could find a flaw in the wording of the indictment it failed and, for this reason until modern times, a prisoner was not allowed to see it prior to the commencement of his or her trial.

Justices of the peace
They heard criminal complaints brought to them by victims and constables and decided if the suspects should be sent for trial or released.

King's evidence
Where a person confessed his guilt of a crime and offered evidence against his co-accused on condition that the charge against him would be dropped he was said to have turned "King's evidence". (Currently Queen's evidence).

Misdemeanour
A minor crime, not punishable by death. Most were tried at Quarter Sessions and only a few at the Old Bailey.

Nullification
The jury's power to acquit a defendant on the basis of conscience even when, on the evidence and the law, the defendant was technically guilty.

Old Bailey
The Assize court for London and Middlesex. (Now a Crown Court).

Pardon
Either a free pardon by the crown under which the convict would receive no punishment or a conditional pardon whereby a sentence

would be reduced as, for example, from the death penalty to transportation.

Partial verdict
The reduction by the jury of the value of money or goods stolen. The reduction in value was often considerable and this **pious perjury** was invoked to prevent widespread use of the death penalty for theft and was largely supported by the public and the judiciary.

Presumption of innocence
The fundamental rule of criminal procedure that the prosecution is obliged to prove its case against an accused person beyond reasonable doubt.

Pro bono publico
Counsel appearing for a defendant without fee, "for the public good".

Shilling
Equivalent of 12 old pence—now five new pence.

Statute
An Act passed by both houses of Parliament and approved by the monarch.

"Thief-taker"
A person who received payment from the government for arresting thieves or arranging the return of stolen goods. Also known as a bounty hunter who, to obtain a reward, would often accuse an innocent person of committing a crime and secure his or her arrest and prosecution. In trials in which Garrow appeared for the defence

in such cases he mercilessly cross-examined them.

Transportation
Sending convicts to serve their sentence overseas, first to the West Indies, then North America and later Australia. By the Transportation Act 1718 a felon guilty of a capital offence subject to benefit of clergy could be transported instead of being sentenced to death.

Treason Trials Act 1696
The statute which, *inter alia,* allowed prisoners accused of treason to have counsel appear for them fully and not merely on points of law. It provided the first step in the birth of adversary trial.

Glossary 2

Capital Offences Tried Frequently at the Old Bailey in Garrow's Time

In London and Middlesex in the period under review indictable offences punishable with death were dealt with at the Old Bailey and included the following:[1]

Assault
Physical attacks on others which included cases where there was no physical attack but the victim was terrified by gestures or shouting.

Assault with intent to rape
Arose where an attempted rape was unsuccessful or it was thought impossible to prove an actual rape.

Bigamy
Marrying a second spouse while the first spouse was still alive.

---

1. See Internet. www.oldbaileyonline.org/history/crime/crimes.html.

Burglary
Breaking into a dwelling-house at night with intent to commit a felony or actually doing so. Such breaking during the hours of daylight was housebreaking.

Housebreaking
If the inhabitants of the house were put in fear.

Coining
Counterfeiting or interfering with the currency of the realm, either coin or paper. The offence included the possession of moulds for the manufacture of coins.

Constructive treason
A doctrine — invented by the judges — that a conspiracy to do some act in regard to the monarch which might endanger his or her life was itself treason, even though not defined as such by statute until the Treason Act 1795.

Customs offences
Included smuggling, seizing goods from customs and excise officers and obstructing or shooting at the officers when performing their duty.

Embezzlement
Thefts committed by clerks, servants or employees of goods belonging to, or in the security of, their employers.

Felony
At common law every serious crime, and many minor offences, were felonies. The penalty was the gallows. The term is now redundant.

Forgery
The fraudulent making or altering of a written document (usually money but also bonds and wills) to the detriment of another.

Fraud
Criminal deceit or false representation, usually obtaining goods under false pretences.

Highway robbery
A robbery on or near the King's highway, which included London streets.

Infanticide
The killing of a new born child. If the accused was an unmarried mother and the death of the baby was concealed the mother had by statute to rebut a presumption of guilt. Generally, however, a mother would be acquitted if she could demonstrate that she had prepared for the birth of the baby, for example by acquiring clothing for it.

Larceny
Was either **simple grand larceny** which was theft of goods of a value of 12 pence or more without aggravating circumstances or **petty larceny** which was theft of goods valued at less than 12 pence and was not a capital crime. **Grand larceny,** where theft of goods valued at 12 pence or more was accompanied by aggravating circumstances, was a capital offence whilst petty larceny, a misdemeanour, was punishable with whipping, imprisonment or transportation.

Libel
The malicious defamation of a person in print in order to expose that person to public hatred. Libels against the monarch were prosecuted

as the more serious offence of **seditious libel.**

Manslaughter
An unlawful killing without premeditation or malice.

Murder
Unlawful homicide with malice aforethought. Where death was caused by an unlawful act done with intention to cause death or bodily harm, or which was commonly known to cause death or bodily harm.

Perjury
Wilfully testifying falsely under oath in a judicial proceeding or procuring another to do so.

Perverting justice
Enticing thieves to commit a crime and then receiving rewards for their arrest and prosecution.

Pickpocketing
Stealing from the person of another, without his knowledge, goods or money worth more than one shilling. It ceased to be a capital offence in 1808.

Rape
Forced sexual intercourse with a woman against her will.

Receiving stolen goods
By a statute of 1691 a person receiving stolen goods, knowing them to be stolen, was guilty of being accessory to a felony.

Returning from transportation
Doing so before the period of the sentence of the court has expired was a felony punishable with death.

Riot
Where three or more persons assembled to carry out an unlawful act, usually to commit a breach of the peace, and then performed it. Where there was an assembly with the intent but no act was performed the charge was **unlawful assembly.**

Royal pardon
After a person was convicted of a capital offence, if the judge (or sometimes the jury) considered that for sound reasons he or she should be shown clemency they could petition the monarch for a royal pardon. This was often done to avoid capital punishment.

Robbery
An open and violent assault to forcibly take property of any value from the victim and putting him or her in fear.

Shoplifting
Stealing goods valued at five shillings or more from a shop.

Treason
Conspiring to overthrow the monarch or levying war against him or her. By the Treason Act of 1352[2] an overt act and two witnesses were required.

---

2. Edw. 3. st. 5, c. 2.

Bibliogaphy

B

Beattie, J M (1991), "Garrow for the Defense", *History Today*, History Today Ltd.

    (1991) "Scales of Justice: Defense Counsel and the English Criminal Trial in the Eighteenth and Nineteenth Centuries", 9(2) *Law and History Review,* Illinois: University of Illinois Press.

Blackstone, Sir William (1830), *Commentaries on the Law of England,* vol. vi. London, Thomas Tegg.

C

Cairns, D J A (1998), Advocacy and the Making of the Adversarial Criminal Trial, 1800-1865, Oxford: The Clarendon Press.

Campbell, Lord John (1868), *Lives of the Chancellors,* vol. vi, London: John Murray.

Crim Con!! Damages Fifteen Thousand Pounds! (1814), "Case of Lord Rosebery Against Sir Henry Mildmay for Criminal Conversation with his Wife", London: John Fairburn.

D

Dwyer, D (2003), "Review of John H Langbein's *The Origins of Adversary Criminal Trial*", 66 *The Modern Law Review*.

E

Euer, Sampson (1677), *Doctrina Placitandi,* London: R & E Atkins.

F

Fox, Lionel W (1952), *The English Prison and Borstal Systems,* London: Routledge & Kegan Paul Ltd.

G

Green, J R (1874), *A Short History of the English People,* London: The Folio Society.

H

Hansard (1833).

Hostettler, John and Braby, Richard (2010), *Sir William Garrow: His Life, Times and Fight for Justice,* Hook, Hampshire: Waterside Press.

K

King, Peter (1988), "Illiterate Plebeians, Easily Misled: Jury Composition, Experience and Behaviour in Essex 1735-1815". In Cockburn, JS and Green, TA, *Twelve Good Men and True: The Criminal Trial Jury in England 1200-1800,* New Jersey: Princeton University Press (2000). *Crime, Justice and Discretion in England 1736-1753,* Oxford: Oxford University Press.

L

Law Review (1844-45).

Linebaugh, Peter (1993), *The London Hanged: Crime and Civil Society in the Eighteenth Century,* London: Penguin Books.

Longford, Elizabeth (1969-72), *Wellington: The Years of the Sword,* London: Weidenfeld & Nicolson.

M

May, Allyson N (2003), *The Bar and the Old Bailey, 1750-1850,* Chapel Hill and London: University of North Carolina Press.

N

Norton, Rictor, *Homosexuality in Eighteenth-Century England.* http://rictornorton.co.uk/eighteen/jones2.htm.

O

Old Bailey Proceedings Online. www.oldbaileyonline.org

P

Pickard, Liz (2005), *Victorian London: The Life of a City 1840-1870,* London: Weidenfeld & Nicolson.

R

Radzinowicz, Leon (1956), *A History of the Criminal Law: The Enforcement of the Law,* London: Stevens & Sons Ltd, vol. ii. P.57.

Robertson, Geoffrey QC (2010), Foreword in John Hostettler and Richard Braby, *Sir William Garrow: His Life, Times and Fight for Justice,* Hook, Hampshire: Waterside Press.

S

State Trials (1821), Stephen, James Fitzjames (1883), *A History of the Criminal Law of England,* London: Macmillan, vol.1.

T

The Observer (1796; 1797).
The Times (4 November 1834; 7 November 1840).
Thorne, R G (1986), *The History of Parliament: The House of Commons 1790-1820*, vol. iv. Members G-P, London: Secker & Warburg.

V

Vogler, Richard (2005), *A World View of Criminal Justice,* Aldershot: Ashgate Publishers.

Index

A
abuse *54*
accomplices *66, 87*
Adams, John *32*
Admiralty *74*
adultery *73, 77*
adversary trial *31, 33, 34, 49, 56, 67, 97, 99, 101, 106*
advocacy *30, 48*
Age of Enlightenment *36*
aggression *29, 70, 84*
amicus curiae *71*
Anderson, Clive *xxi, 28*
anti-establishment *xii*
appeal *61*
aristocracy *xvii*
  aristocratic connections *35*
armed uprising *66*
Armstrong, Alun *xviii*
artistic licence *67*
assault with intent to rape *107*
Assizes *xviii, 44, 101*
Associations for the Prosecution of Felons *101*
atrocity *72*
Attorney-General *xiv, 81, 94, 97, 102*
attorneys *73*
Australia *32, 106*

B
BAFTA nomination *xx*
Baillie, Captain *74*
Bambridge, Matthew *84*
barristers *28*
Bartlett, William *89*
BBC *27, 29, 53, 97, 99*
bear-baiters *42*
bear-garden *46, 65*
Beattie, John M *xvii, 29, 40*
Bedlam *84*
Bellingham, John *83*
benefit of clergy *46, 102*
bigamy *107*
"Billingsgate Boy" *xiii, 28, 55, 60, 98*
Bill of Rights (USA) *35*
black

black cloth *76*
"Black Sessions" *55*
blackmail *73*
Blackstone, Sir William *31, 85*
Blake, William *42*
blasphemy *34*
blood money *43, 65*
bludgeon men *42*
blue plaque *xxii*
bounty hunters *43, 102, 105*
Braby, Richard *vii, xvi, 58*
Bramber, West Sussex *68*
branding *46, 102*
brawling *30*
breach of the peace *111*
breaking and entering *77*
breaking looms *84*
Bremner, Ann *xxiii*
Brixham *67*
Brougham, Henry *60, 78*
Buchan, Andrew *xviii*
Buller, Judge/Mr Justice *xviii, 56, 57, 81, 85*
bullying *30*
burglary *42, 108*

C
"cab-rank" rule *62*
Calabar *94*
Calderon, Luisa *93*
Cambridge *28*

Campbell, Lord John *84*
Canada *32*
capital offences *35, 43, 55, 102*
Casson, Nicholas *95*
cell interviews *57*
cesspits *41*
character
good character *71*
chariot harness *58*
charity work *98*
chattels
slaves as chattels *72*
Cheapside *28, 48, 55*
Cheeseman, Mary *45*
Chesum, Samuel *39*
children *76, 99*
China *32*
citizen's arrest *96*
civil liberties *98*
clemency *111*
Coachmaker's Hall *47*
coarseness *30*
Code of Conduct of the English Bar *63*
coining *42, 108*
Cole, Edgar *62*
colonial rule *93*
common law *32, 36, 102*
confessions *39, 103*
conscience *85, 104*
contagion *55*

contradictions *95*
convention *xii*
conviction *xiii*, *38*, *43*, *64*, *94*
corruption *xii*, *42*, *74*
  noble cause corruption *xii*
counsel *43*, *46*
  "no-counsel" rule *34*, *48*
counterfeiting *108*
courage *47*
court
  Court of Common Pleas *89*
  "sordid court" *31*
courtroom *27*, *28*, *33*, *35*, *47*
  courtroom scene *55*
Courts Act 1971 *101*
Covent Garden *95*
Crawfurd, Arthur *vii*, *xxiii*
credibility *34*
Crespigny, William Champion *58*
Crim Con!! *78*
crime/criminal *41*
  criminal code *32*
  criminal conversation *77*
  "criminal districts" *42*
  criminal justice system *32*
  criminal law *28*
Crompton, Richard *60*
cross-examination *xv*, *xix*, *30*, *35*, *37*, *49*, *55*, *57*, *63*, *71*, *84*, *89*, *103*
  aggressive cross-examination *38*
crown *53*, *104*
Crown Courts *101*
cruelty *42*
Culkin, Michael *xviii*
customs offences *108*
cutting flesh *60*
cutting silk *84*

D

Daily Telegraph *xxi*
damages *77*
dark side *98*
Davis, John *76*
debate *xxi*
  debating societies *47*
Declaration of the Rights of Man *35*
defamation *75*, *109*
delusion *82*, *83*
depositions *54*, *64*
deprivation *31*, *41*
deranged soldier *81*
detention during the pleasure of the crown *83*
diminished responsibility *84*
Dingler, George *37*
discretion *45*
dispossession *62*
divine imprimatur *34*
Dixon, Robert *44*

dock *103*
Doctors' Commons *73*
Doctrina Placitandi *60*
Dore, Sarah (Lady Sarah Hill) *xviii, xxiii, 49, 53, 61*
doubt *37*
drama *27*
   dramatic impact *xii*
Drury Lane Theatre *81*
duel *58*
due process *32*
Duke of Wellington *77*
Duke of York *82*
Durston, Gregory *xvii*

E

ecclesiastical courts *73*
Edward 1 *34*
eloquence *70*
embezzlement *108*
Enlightenment *36*
Enoch, Thomas *65*
Episode 1 *54*
Episode 3 *58*
equity *77*
Erskine, Thomas *53, 63, 67, 69, 70, 75, 78, 81, 97*
Essex *86*
evidence *33, 36*
   "Best evidence" rule *102*
   false testimony *xiii*
   law of evidence *40*
   planted evidence *66, 68*
   precarious or uncertain evidence *37*
   rules of evidence *33*
   "second-hand evidence" *38*
examination-in-chief *103*
execution *43, 87*
extemporisation *27*

F

fact *27*
Fairford, Viscount *77*
false prosecutions *102*
false testimony *xiii*
Farmer, John *73*
felony *30, 31, 34, 35, 43, 108*
   felony trials *35*
fetters *93*
fiction *27, 53*
Fighting for Justice *xiv*
flash coachmen *42*
forensic battle *33*
forgery *109*
Forrester, Edward *54, 56, 65*
Foster Lane *48*
Fox, Charles James *95*
Fox, Lionel W *55*
France *32*
franchise reform *69*
fraud *96, 109*

French Revolution *36*, *68*, *70*
frenzy *82*

G
gallows *43*, *44*, *45*, *85*
game laws *58*
gaol fever *55*, *65*
Garrow
  Dr David William Garrow *vii*, *61*
  "Garrow's Law" *x*, *27*, *53*
  Garrow Society *xxii*
  William Garrow *xi*, *27*, *53*
    achievements *29*
    airbrushed from history *27*
    "Counsellor Garrow" *48*
    first case *54*
    Garrow as a judge *xiv*, *97*
    genius *98*
    images *xxiii*
    lack of legal knowledge *xxiv*, *59*
    Member of Parliament *97*
    reactionary Tory in later life *98*
George III *81*
Georgia *32*
Germany *32*
gerrymandering *42*
gestures *107*
Gibb, Francis *xxi*

Glorious Revolution *34*
goal fever *xvii*
golden rules of the Bar *63*
good and evil *81*
good character *71*
grand jury *86*
Graves, Rupert *xviii*
Great Terror *36*
Greenwich Hospital for Seamen *74*
Grose, Mr Justice *88*
Grove, William *54*, *55*
grubbers *42*
"guinea men" *xiii*
Gunpowder Plot *67*

H
habeus corpus *66*, *103*
Hadfield, James *81*
Hale, Sir Matthew *89*
Hamer, Joseph *66*
Hamer, Mary *68*
hanging *56*, *65*, *84*
Hannay, John Bean *94*
hard labour *87*
hardship *43*
Hardy, Thomas *66*, *70*
harlots *42*
Hayward, William *58*
health
  ill-health *32*

hearsay *37, 59, 68, 102, 103*
Heath, Mr Justice *89*
helplessness *43*
Henry I *45*
Henry II *46, 102*
Hertfordshire *86*
High Court *53, 81*
highwaymen *49*
highway robbery *46, 54, 64*
Hill, Sir Arthur *xviii, 56, 73, 77*
  fact and fiction *61*
History of the Criminal Law of
  England *31*
Hogarth *42*
Holdsworth, Sir William *31*
Holland *42*
Holroyd, Mr Justice *94*
Home Secretary *62*
Homicide Act 1957 *83*
Hompesch, Baron *58*
Hood, Lord *95*
horse stealing *42*
Hostettler, John *ix, xiv*
Hotham, Baron *38*
housebreaking *77, 108*
House of Commons *102*
house of correction *87*
House of Lords *76*
human rights *29, 35, 70, 98*
hustings *95*

I

identification *56, 84, 102*
idiocy *89*
illiteracy *32*
imprisonment *43, 109*
incarceration *43*
incense *55, 65*
India *32*
indictment *34, 54, 64, 103*
inducement *39, 103*
infanticide *56, 109*
injustice *35, 54, 76*
innocence *43*
  presumption of innocence
    xviii, 33, 36, 43, 105
  absence of *56*
inquisitorial system *36*
insanity *81*
inspiration *29*
insults *55*
insurance claim *72*
interpreters *89*
invention *27*
Italy *32*

J

Jamaica *88*
Jarvis, Elizabeth *56*
Jasker, David *73*
Jefferson, Thomas *32*
Jones, Captain Robert *73*

Jones, Elizabeth *86*
Jones, William *38*
judge *89*
  as an umpire *57*
  domineering judges *xii*
  Garrow as a judge *xiv*, *97*
  hostile judges *33*
  iron hand of the judiciary *33*
  lesser role in trials *57*
judiciary *37*
jurists *31*
jury *43*, *46*, *49*, *54*, *65*
  addressing the jury *31*
  bending the rules *84*
  empathy with *70*
  habitual, prosecution-minded, jurors *xii*
  jury nullification *57*, *85*
  "playing the jury like a harpist" *84*
  speeches to the jury not allowed *56*
  trial by jury *34*, *99*
justice *54*
  justices of the peace *104*
  "pantomime of justice" *76*
juxtaposition *xi*

K
Kent *86*
Kenyon, Lord *81*

kidnapping *94*
King, Peter *48*, *86*
King's Bench *75*
King's Counsel *xv*, *69*
King's evidence *85*, *104*

L
larceny *85*, *109*
Latin America *32*
law *54*
  law French *60*
  Law Lords *83*
  Law Magazine *47*
  Law of Pleading *60*
  Law Society Gazette *xxi*
  mercy of the law *81*
  point of law *59*
lawyers *57*, *69*
  defence lawyers *27*
leading questions *103*
legal
  legal help *43*
  legal rules *54*
  legal techniques *30*
legitimacy *47*
lèse majesté *34*
libel *109*
liberty *40*, *69*
life *40*
Lincoln's Inn *28*, *48*, *54*, *60*
London *107*

City of London *46*
London Corresponding Society *68*
London life *27*
London's Monster *59*
trading hub *41*
Lord Chancellor *97*
Lucas, Richard *96*
Lynam, Charles *68*

M
madness
raving madness *82*
magistrates/magistrates' court *44, 54, 64*
malice aforethought *110*
Mansfield, Lord *75*
manslaughter *83, 110*
Marchant, Tony *xi, 27*
Margate *99*
marriage *73*
Marshall, Lyndsey *xviii*
May, Allyson *30*
Melville, Viscount *68, 96*
menace *39*
mercy *83, 85*
Merryman, John *87*
mezzotint *xxiv*
Middle Ages *46*
Middlesex *46, 107*
Milk Street *28, 55*

miscarriages of justice *48*
misdemeanour *104*
Mitford, Sir John *81*
mitigation of punishments *47*
M'Naghten Rules *83*
Morocco men *42*
mudlarks *42*
murder *37, 43, 46, 57, 65, 72, 95, 110*
constructive murder *96*

N
Napoleon Bonaparte *36*
National Gallery *xxiv*
National History Museum *93*
necessity *72*
"neck verse" *46, 102*
negligence *72*
Newgate Prison *xvii, 55*
New Zealand *32*
Nicholson, Patrick *95*
Nigeria *94*
North America *106*
nullification *104*
jury nullification *57, 85*

O
oath *33, 34, 91*
conflict of oaths *34*
Old Bailey *27, 31, 33, 35, 39, 41, 45, 53, 101, 104*

"Old Bailey Hacks" 30
Old Bailey Sessions Papers 46
sordid atmosphere 70
oppression 36
oratory 47
ordeal 34
Oxford xxiv, 28

P
Pace, Peter 54, 55
Pagan, "Sir John" 41
Pallis, Mark xviii
pardon 104
royal pardon 111
Parliament 35
Pearson, Sarah 88
Pegwell Bay 99
Pegwell Bay/Cottage xxii
Perceval, Spencer 83
perjury 35, 43, 54, 66, 102, 110
"pious perjury" xii, 84
perquisites 59
Perryn, Baron 95
persecution 34
perverting justice 110
pestilence 55
petty crime 46
Philanthropic Society 98
Pickering, William 87
pickpocketing 41, 110
Picton, General Thomas 93

pillory 60
pioneer xiii
Pitt, Sarah 59
Pitt, William 67, 70, 98
poignancy 53
police 42, 95
absence of 64
politicians 34, 56
poor house 42
population
teeming population 41
Porter, Ann 59
poverty xvii, 41, 99
power 42
precedent 34
prejudice xi, 33
Prince of Wales 58
prison
legal visits 59
seeing clients in jail xi, 49
prisoners 31
health 41
pro bono publico 87, 105
promise 39
proof
burden/onus of proof 56
prosecution
paranoid prosecutions 98
prostitutes 42
Protestantism 67
Pugh, Phoebe 65

punishment
   draconian punishments *xi*

Q
Queen's evidence *104*
Quinn and Foley *84*

R
radicals *xii, 98*
Radio Times *xiii*
Radnell, Eliza *54, 63*
Radzinowicz, Leon *31*
Ramsgate *49, 99*
rank *42*
rape *34, 46, 62, 110*
   rape of a servant *62*
Rasten, John *89*
Rawlings, Thomas *69*
reasonable doubt *36*
rebels *xii*
receiving stolen goods *38, 110*
"reign of terror" *66*
relationship *61*
revolution *28*
   French Revolution *36*
rewards *xiii, 105*
   government rewards *54*
   private rewards *65, 101*
Rex v Baillie *75*
rights
   Declaration of the Rights of Man *35*
   defendant's rights *29*
   prisoners' rights *36*
riots *95, 111*
robbery *41, 55, 65, 111*
   highway robbery *109*
Robertson, Geoffrey QC *xix, 98*
romantic interest *61*
Rosebery, Lord *78*
rotten boroughs *68, 97*
Royal Humane Society *98*
royal pardon *47, 73, 111*
Royal Sea Bathing Infirmary *99*
Royal Television Society Award *xx*
ruffians *30*
ruling class *xiii*
rulings of the Bench *29*
Russell, John RA *vii, xxiii*
Russell, Lord John *70*
Russia *32, 36*

S
sabotage *84*
Sanders of Oxford *xxiv*
Sandwich, Lord *74*
scandal *78*
Scotland *xxiv, 70*
Scott, Sir John *68*
scuffle hunters *42*
Seamen's Hospital case *74*

secrecy *36*
sedition *66*
  seditious libel *110*
self-incrimination *38*
sentence of death *56, 76, 85, 105*
Series 1 *53*
Series 2 *71*
Series 3 *81*
Serjeant's Inn *40*
servants' rights *59*
sewage *41*
Sherwood *58*
shipwrecked people *98*
shoplifting *42, 86, 111*
shouting *107*
sign language *89*
silence
  by the accused *59*
Silvester, John *xiii, 38, 55, 58, 68, 72, 78*
skills *70*
  forensic skills *30*
Slade, Sarah *87*
slavery *72, 92*
  anti-slavery movement *xvii*
  moral issue of slavery *94*
  Slavery Emancipation Act 1833 *94*
  Slave Trade Abolition Act 1807 *94*
Smith, Mary *86*

smuggling *108*
sodomy *73*
solicitors *28, 54*
  Solicitor-General *97*
Southouse, William *xviii, 28, 54, 73*
Spain *32*
spectators *55, 65*
speeches
  speech to the jury *xix, 65*
speed of justice *46*
spies *69*
Spitalfields Mill *84*
"spouting" *xxii, 47*
Stalin *36*
standards
  low standards *30*
Stanton, Katherine *65*
state *98*
  power of the state *29*
  state trials *xiv, 53, 68, 70, 97*
station in life *42*
statute *105*
Steele, Sam *66*
Stephen, James Fitzjames *31*
stereotypes *xxiv*
stocks *66*
strolling minstrels *42*
Stubbs, Robert *72*
subjugation *92*
subpoena *55*

Suffield, Lord *76, 77*
suicide *61*
Surrey *86*
Sussex *86*
"sweepings" *44, 58*

T

tension *xix, 27, 61*
terror *66*
　"English Terror" *70*
　French Terror *67*
Thayer, James Bradley *31*
theft *39, 45, 58, 63, 65, 71, 93*
　theft from the Royal Mail *76*
The Times *xxi, 47*
"thief-takers" *xiii, 43, 54, 64, 84, 102, 105*
threat *39, 103*
thugs *30*
timidity *48*
Tingay, James *45*
Tollin, Mary *62, 63*
Tories *98*
torture *33, 36, 92, 93*
Tower Hamlets *95*
trade union *84*
transformation *31*
transportation *43, 44, 47, 66, 81, 85, 87, 91, 94, 105, 106, 109*
　returning without lawful excuse *88, 111*

Transportation Act 1718 *106*
treason *34, 111*
　constructive treason *108*
　high treason *66, 81*
　Treason Act 1352 *111*
　Treason Act 1795 *108*
　treason trials *34, 35*
　Treason Trials Act 1696 *34, 106*
trial *29, 57*
　English method of criminal trial *29*
　Picton trial *92*
　trial by jury *34*
Trinidad *92, 93*
troops *66*
truth *28*
Tudor times *102*
typhoid *41*
typhus *55*

U

Ukraine *32*
underdog *49*
underworld *xiii*
United States of America *32*
university *28*
unlawful assembly *111*

V

value of property *66*
verdict *71*

partial verdict *86, 105*
vested interest *xiii*
victims *62*
vigour *47*
violence *41, 65*
Vogler, Richard *xvii, 33*

W

warrants *66, 69*
wealth *42, 56*
West End *42*
West Indies *72, 92, 93, 106*
Westminster *95*
West Sussex *68*
Whigs *34*
whipping *87, 109*
White, Nicholas *77*
Wiley, Thomas *76*
William of Orange *67*
Williams, Renwick *59*
Wilson, Margaret *39*
witnesses *33, 34, 60, 76, 82, 103*
  compliant witnesses *xii*
  hostile witnesses *70*
  witnesses to character *55*
women
  benefit of clergy *102*
  women's rights *54, 62*
Wood, Mary *87*
Wray, Sir Cecil *95*
Wright, Sir Sampson *96*

Wynford, Lord *77*

Z

Zong Slave Ship case *72*

The Garrow Society

The Garrow Society was formed to advance discussion about 18th and 19th century English lawyer William Garrow. Society members include researchers, authors, legal experts, direct descendants of Garrow, lawyers, and those with a general interest.

Content includes:
- Garrow Trials
- Family Stories
- The Campaign to Save Garrow's Marine Villa
- Links to TV, Books and Film
- Forum

We welcome new members—please register in order to contribute to the discussion, take part in the forums or add to the genealogical data.

Go to
www.garrowsociety.org

Sir William Garrow
His Life, Times and Fight for Justice
John Hostettler and Richard Braby
Foreword Geoffrey Robertson QC

The true story of the central character in the BBC prime-time drama 'Garrow's Law'.

Written by historian and biographer John Hostettler and family storyteller Richard Braby (a descendent of Garrow).

'A blockbuster of a book'
Phillip Taylor

'A delight'
Internet Law Book Reviews

Extent	352 pages
Format	Paperback
Published	January 2011
ISBN	978-1-904380-69-6

WatersidePress.co.uk/SWG